Chronicle of My Mother

Chronicle of My Mother

Yasushi Inoue

Translated by
Jean Oda Moy

KODANSHA INTERNATIONAL LTD.
Tokyo, New York and San Francisco

Distributed in the United States by Kodansha International/USA Ltd., through Harper & Row, Publishers, Inc., 10 East 53rd Street, New York, New York 10022.

Published by Kodansha International Ltd., 12-21, Otowa 2-chome, Bunkyo-ku, Tokyo 112 and Kodansha International/USA Ltd., with offices at 10 East 53rd Street, New York, New York 10022 and The Hearst Building, 5 Third Street, Suite No. 430, San Francisco, California 94103.

LCC 82-48292
ISBN 0-87011-533-2
ISBN 4-7700-1045-1 (in Japan)

CONTENTS

INTRODUCTION

In the autobiographical *Chronicle of My Mother*, Yasushi Inoue, one of Japan's foremost novelists, portrays with great sensitivity and compassion the universal experience of adult children dealing with aging parents as he follows his own mother's aging and senility. Although the account concerns a particular Japanese family, anyone who has had close contact with the elderly will recognize the behavior and interaction of successive generations since the problems of aging are universal.

The book comprises three sections, each of which was originally written and published as a separate, complete work: "Under the Blossoms" (1964); "The Light of the Moon" (1969); "The Surface of the Snow" (1974). As the author explains in the opening lines of "The Light of the Moon," the collected version, like each of the sections, is neither novel nor essay in form. It is rather a series of vignettes, chronological observations made by the author while he recorded the events accompanying his mother's inexorable decline. There are no climaxes in this chronicle;

the sequences are more like the ebb and flow of the tide, with the family gathering and dispersing, conferring and observing, as it shares and contemplates the mysteries of the final phase of life.

In a private conversation Inoue strongly voiced his feeling that this work "was my intention to protect my mother and prevent anyone from ridiculing her." He further stated that the result is one of his favorites among his own books, and after the last section was completed he felt he had nothing left to say to his mother. His love for her is implicit throughout, and it is my impression that the act of writing served as the author's personal catharsis, his way of dealing with his grief as well as formulating his tribute and farewell.

In the more general perspective, this is also a story of how the members of one Japanese family—especially the women—assumed responsibility for the care of their matriarch in her decline and how they dealt with the frustrations, doubts, and concerns that went with that responsibility. Their acceptance of and gentleness toward her, even when she was at her most trying, their constant attempts to understand what might be going on in her wandering mind, and their periodic discussions aimed at explaining her behavior to each other: all this bespeaks a filial love and compassion that is truly moving.

Despite Inoue's own emotional involvement with his subject, he is able to step back to record detailed observations about the process of his mother's senility and the concomitant family interactions. His observations are never coldly clinical, however. Indeed, his professional beginnings as a poet are never more clearly evident than in the imagery he evokes when taking the long view, particularly in the passages that highlight the titles of each section. Note, for instance, the powerfully juxtaposed images of the mother-son relationship at two different times and ages "in the piercing light of the moon."

With the unprecedented social and cultural changes taking place in Japan today, many traditional values which might appear to interfere with productivity and "success"—in short, with rampant materialism—are losing ground. Many of Japan's aged now are less fortunate than the author's mother, whose family adhered to the Confucian ideal of honoring and cherishing the old. In Japan as in the West, the elderly today are frequently shunted aside, ignored, or made to feel they are a burden. A sad commentary of this state of affairs is that at special temples for the aged in Japan, penitants increasingly pray for early death. In such times as these, it is refreshing to share the experience of one loving, responsive family.

This book will be received as a treasure by those who appreciate superb reflective writing. In addition, it should be of special interest to sociologists, gerontologists, and persons engaged in family studies. It will have special appeal, of course, for those Asian Americans who have been instilled with Confucian values, and for those more distantly removed, who wish to renew their ties with their own cultural heritage. It can also be of value to anyone who has experienced or is currently undergoing a similar family situation: for them it will lend much understanding and affirmation that they are not alone in dealing with the painful life dilemma of how to give support to those who nurtured them in the past.

This translation is dedicated to the memory of my own mother, Chieko Nakamoto Oda, who gave me love and sustenance during my early years and to whom I reciprocated with support and caring in her decline.

Jean Oda Moy

Sunnyvale, California, 1982

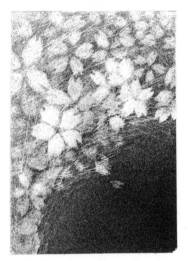

Under
the
Blossoms

Five years ago Father died. He was eighty. At the age of forty-eight, as soon as he attained the rank of brigadier general in the Army Medical Corps, Father retired and withdrew to his home village in Izu. There, for over thirty years, he cultivated a small plot in back of the house and passed his days working at growing enough vegetables to feed himself and Mother. At the age he left the army he could easily have established a practice for himself, but he had no such inclination. With the Pacific War in 1942, military hospitals and convalescent homes sprang up everywhere, and due to the shortage of military doctors he was asked several times to become a director of one of them. But Father spurned every offer, giving his age as a reason. It seemed that once he had doffed his military uniform he had no desire to wear it ever again. He had his army pension and did not want for food, although material goods were in short supply. Had he been connected with a hospital, it is certain that my parents' somber life-style, which was verging toward indigence, would have been quite different. Not only would they have had financial resources but contact with others would have given some stimulation to the lives of these two old people.

On one occasion I actually returned to our home village for the express purpose of persuading Father to take up the offer from a military hospital after learning about it from Mother's letters. However, I left without even speaking to him about it. Somehow, after Father entered his sixties, his frail and diminishing figure—as he moved about his backyard plot in patched work clothes—had suddenly become totally unrelated to society. During the same visit I learned from Mother that one could count the number of times Father left the house since retiring to the village. Although he was friendly enough to people who visited, he did not visit others. Three or four relatives lived a few blocks away, but unless one of them suffered a misfortune Father would not visit them. He was even said to be reluctant to step into the street in front of the house.

My sisters, brother, and I had long known Father was afflicted with a certain misanthropy, but we were not aware how this tendency had intensified while we went about our lives, moving to cities, establishing our own homes, and distancing ourselves from our parents' world.

Since Father was the way he was, it probably never occurred to him to call on his children for help—and indeed he probably could have gotten by on his pension alone had times remained reasonably stable. But the end of the war brought extreme changes, and for a time the pension stopped. When it was resumed, the amount had shrunk and so had the value of money. I began sending Father money each month, which he accepted, although it must have hurt him a lot to do so. He wasted nothing and refused to spend a cent more than was absolutely necessary to maintain the most frugal life-style.

After the war he continued to work his land. He also raised chickens and even made his own miso soybean paste for cooking, so he only spent money for rice. Whenever my sisters, brother, and I got together we would criticize and lament Father's abstemiousness, but we could not get him to change. We, his children, now independent members of society, wanted to make our parents' last years comfortable but, try as we could, money sent to him would not be spent; presents of clothing and bedding would be put away and seldom, if ever, used. The result was that the only thing we could do was to send food. Food would spoil, and rather than let that happen, Father would eat it and allow Mother to have some, too.

I think I could describe Father's eighty years of life as "pure." He bestowed no charity on others and he incurred no enmity. Looking back over his thirty-year retirement, I am convinced that even if he had wanted to, he could not have lived a more worldly life. His savings account after his death revealed only an amount appropriate to cover his and Mother's funeral expenses. He had married into my mother's family and taken her surname, as was common for families that only had a daughter to carry on the family name, and the estate he had inherited was left, intact, to me, his eldest son. It appeared that after the war Father had sold off most of the household furnishings that had been purchased during his military service, so nothing of value remained. However, of the things handed down from generation to generation, such as scrolls and art objects, not a single item was lost. Father had neither increased nor decreased the estate by so much as a penny.

When still young, I left my parents to be raised at the house of a woman I knew as my grandmother. Her name was Nui, and although I called her grandmother we had no blood ties. She had been a mistress of my great-grandfather, who was a doctor. After his death, Nui's name was formally entered into our family register and she started a branch family with herself as Mother's "foster mother." All this was done according to my great-grandfather's will, and I must say it was quite in character, for he had behaved unconventionally all his life.

Thus, according to the family register Nui was a grandmother of mine. When I was little I called her "Granny Onui," to distinguish her from "Great Granny," my real great-grandmother (who at that time was still living in the main house) and plain "Granny," who was Mother's mother and my real grandmother. There was no particular reason why I was raised by Granny Onui. I was temporarily placed in her home in our village when Mother, pregnant with my sister, found herself without household help. From that time on, I was left to spend my early years with Granny Onui. From her point of view, my presence probably helped consolidate her position in the family, although it would, in any case, have been hard for her to let me go because she was a lonely old woman and genuinely fond of me. As far as I was concerned, since the move took place when I was only five or six and I was very attached to Granny Onui, it was natural that I should not want to return home. And for my parents' part, with my brother's birth following my sister's, they felt no urgency to bring me back—especially since I resisted so much.

Granny Onui died when I was a sixth grader in elementary school. After her death I left the village for the first time to enter the family comprising my parents, my brother, and my sisters, and to enroll in middle school at my father's post. With his next transfer, however, after less than a year, my life with my family ended once again. I transferred to a school in a small town near our village and had to live in a dormitory. I was to spend a total of two more years with my family, one year after middle school and one year when I was in high school, until Father's transfer again interfered. From that time on I never lived with my parents or brother and sisters again.

Even though I was a child not destined to live with Father, he made no distinction at all between me and the three children he raised under his roof. He was fair in all situations, not through forcing himself but because it was not his nature to feel more attachment for one child than for another. The same could be said of all his other relatives. If one were to line them up, together with his children, it would be almost uncanny to see his impartiality in dispensing affection. Indeed, there seemed to be a part of him that could not tell the difference between one of his own sons or daughters and a veritable stranger. Thus to his children he seemed very distant, while he struck new acquaintances as a warm person.

When Father was seventy he had a cancer, which was successfully removed by surgery. Ten years later, however, the malignancy recurred and he was confined to bed for half a year while his condition gradually deteriorated. Because of his age, surgery was not considered, and death became just a matter of time. Toward the end, for almost a month, we expected each day to be his last. My sisters,

17

brother, and I brought our funeral clothes home and commuted between Tokyo and the village, waiting for the invalid's death. The last time I visited Father the doctor told me he would probably hold out for four or five more days, so I returned that night to Tokyo. But the next day, during my absence, Father drew his last breath. He was clearheaded to the very end, giving detailed instructions to those around him about what meals to prepare for people who visited him and whom to notify of his death.

The last time I saw him, when I informed him that I was going to Tokyo but would return in two or three days, he took his emaciated right hand out from beneath the bed clothes and reached toward me. Since Father had never done anything like that before, I could not understand what he wanted, but I took his hand in mine. Then Father clasped it. Just that—two hands gently holding onto each other. Then in the next instant I felt my hand being softly pushed away. It was a sensation similar to the slight jerk of the tip of a fishing rod. I was startled and withdrew my hand quickly. I still don't know how to interpret this, but I had the distinct feeling that Father was expressing some deep, inner reaction by this gesture, and at that moment I felt chilled, chastised—as if Father were saying, "You're being arrogant, holding your father's hand. It's no joke," and suddenly I felt rejected.

For some time after Father's death this incident stayed in my mind, and I speculated about it like one obsessed. Perhaps, realizing he was near death, Father had stretched out his hand to express his love for me for the last time as a father and then, suddenly despising such feelings in himself, had pushed my hand away. This seemed to be the most plausible explanation. But perhaps it was not so. Perhaps Father had sensed something amiss in my response, and thus had immediately withdrawn the love he was trying to express and let go of my hand. In either case, there was no doubt that in the almost imperceptible way he pushed my hand away our brief moment of closeness gave way to our usual distance. Such an action, I thought, would be altogether typical of him, and therefore I ought to accept it.

Yet, on the other hand, I could not rid myself of a nagging doubt. Perhaps *I* was the one who had pushed away *his* hand, just as I had thought it possible that he had let go of my hand. Perhaps any rebuff between us originated from me. I had no basis for denying it. "At this stage, it's not like you to behave like a child with me," I might have felt. "You shouldn't stretch out your hand to someone like me, your child." And, as a reaction, I might have pushed away the hand I had just clasped. I was deeply distressed whenever this possibility intruded on my thoughts.

Finally, I was released from endless musing over this small, last incident between us. It happened quite suddenly and unexpectedly. One day it occurred to me that in his grave Father, like me, might be pondering the meaning of that secret, barely perceptible interchange. Suddenly I felt free. With this fantasy I felt like my father's child for the first time, something that had never happened during his lifetime. I knew: I am my father's child, and he is my father.

After Father's death, I was frequently struck by my resemblance to him in many ways. While he was alive the thought never occurred to me, assured as I was by those around me that I had a totally different personality. From the time I was a student I consciously willed myself not to think like Father, not to behave like him, although it would have been hard to find any similarity between us. Father was a misanthrope from his youth, whereas I always had many friends, was an athlete during my student days, and genuinely liked to be in the center of things. This gregariousness stayed with me after I left university and entered the real world, and when I myself reached the age at which Father had retired I did not consider the possibility of withdrawing to the village and shutting myself away. After my mid-forties I left the newspaper company I was working in to make a fresh start as a writer, the same age Father had cut off all connections with society.

Yet after Father died I would feel him inside me at odd moments. Sometimes when stepping off the veranda into the garden, for example, or groping for my garden slippers, I would feel that I had taken on the same mannerisms as Father. I had similar feelings when I spread out the newspapers in the living room and bent over to read them. There were times when I would pick up a pack of cigarettes, become aware that I was going through some of the same gestures as Father, and unconsciously set the pack down. In the morning, looking into the bathroom mirror while shaving—rinsing the brush and squeezing the water from it—I would realize, "You are doing exactly what Father did."

Quite apart from the mannerisms, it dawned on me that I might be slipping into Father's way of thinking. When working I frequently get up from my desk to sit on a wicker chair on the veranda, letting my thoughts wander at random, with no connection to the work at hand. At those times I always fix my gaze on the old Chinese ash tree, which has branches spreading out in all directions. One day I recalled that Father also looked out at the branches of a tree as he sat in his wicker chair on the veranda in our country home. I felt then as if I were staring into a deep pool in front of me. I was overawed by the realization that Father had lost himself in thought in the same way. With feelings like these, the image of Father as a distinct and individual human being formed in my mind. I began to see him and talk with him frequently.

I also became aware that one of the roles Father performed in his lifetime was to shield me from death. While he was alive I had the feeling—this was not conscious, it lay somewhere in the back of my mind—that I need not think of my own mortality. But after Father passed away that region lying between myself and death came more into focus; the view was no longer totally obstructed and, like it or not, I had to look at one part of the sea of death. I began to think that my turn would come. Thus I came to realize, only after Father died, that by the mere fact of his living, a father protects his child. This was not something that Father was aware of either; it is simply part of the parent-child relationship, yet it is undoubtedly as elemental as any parental bond.

After Father's death, I started envisaging my own death as an incident perhaps not too far off. However, since Mother was still healthy, the sea of death was half-screened from me, and very different from what it is today. Mother, who is five years younger than Father, is now at the age he was at the time of his death. In other words, she is eighty this year.

The major problem that emerged right after Father's death was what to do with Mother, who was now alone at the country home. Of her four children, one daughter lived in Mishima, while the younger son, the younger daughter, and I all had homes in Tokyo. Mother had no desire whatever to leave her own home. She had lived there for the thirty years of Father's retirement and was very used to it. Her children, however, did not feel she could be left alone for any length of time at her age. Physically, Mother was extremely healthy. She was of slight build, but her back was straight, and after a little activity sometimes her cheeks would take on such a flush that she did not look like an old woman. She was able to read newspapers without glasses, and although she had lost one or two molars she did not have a single false tooth. But for all her vitality, she had grown extremely forgetful, and about two or three years before Father's death she was already beginning to repeat things two or three times. Father had been very anxious about leaving Mother behind, and up to the time of his death he would ask everyone he saw to take care of her.

I had dismissed his fears as exaggerated, but now that Mother was alone I came to understand his concern.

It was hard to detect Mother's senility so long as I was away from her, but after being with her for a while I discovered that it was much worse than I anticipated. In a five- or ten-minute discussion her problem was not obvious, but after an hour or so Mother would utter many word-for-word repetitions. It appeared that she forgot not only her own words as soon as she had spoken them but others' responses as well, and after a while she would raise a topic that had already been discussed. There was nothing odd about the subjects themselves: they would always be very much in character for Mother, who, unlike Father, had been gregarious from youth. Even when inquiring after someone's health, her manner of asking revealed her essential gentleness. As long as one listened to her only once, there was no sign that a part of her brain had become rusted with age. But having to listen longer to the same words and phrases spoken without any change of expression, one could not help noticing her oddness.

Mother lived in the country home with a maid young enough to be her grandchild until the first anniversary of Father's death. After the anniversary funerary ceremony was over, and after much fussing, she reluctantly agreed to move to Tokyo to live with her younger daughter, in other words, my sister Soko. Soko had left the family she married into and was running her own beauty shop. My younger brother and I lived in Tokyo, too, but Mother wanted to be looked after by her daughter rather than by her daughters-in-law. She consented to the move only on condition that she settled in her daughter's home. This was how Soko came to take care of her.

After moving to Tokyo Mother repeated herself with ever greater frequency. Whenever Soko came to my house she spoke of her frustrations in trying to deal with Mother. It must have been an unbearable strain on her, listening to the same phrases repeated like a scratched record from morning till night. Occasionally, to give my sister a breather, I had Mother come over to stay. But invariably, after one night, she would want to return to Soko's. Even when we forced her to stay longer, it was never for even three days. My own family noticed that her forgetfulness and repetitiveness had got worse with each visit.

"Granny is breaking down, isn't she?" my elder son, a university student, once observed, and as I watched Mother she did seem like a malfunctioning machine. She did not look ill, but a part of her was not working—only a part, for the rest was functioning well, which made her all the more difficult to deal with. The broken parts and the functioning parts were so intermingled that it was hard to distinguish between them. Her forgetfulness was very evident, but somewhere there were parts that remembered and did not forget.

When Mother stayed with us, she would come to my study several times a day. I would hear her distinctive slippered steps come pattering down the hall, and I knew Mother was on her way. Presently she would enter and say, very formally, "Excuse me a moment." Then, prefacing her statements with "I have been meaning to discuss this with you," she would bring up a topic we had covered many times. The content of her business was limited to things like "Such-and-such's daughter was married and we must send her a gift," or "So-and-so has said this or that and I want you to know it." For us these were trivial matters, but it was obvious from the way Mother repeated them that they were important to her.

Sometimes on her umpteenth visit to my study, even Mother would wonder if we might not have discussed the matter already, and her expression would betray some uncertainty and hesitancy. At other times, when she started with her "Excuse me . . . ," I would forestall her by saying that I knew what she was about to tell me. Knowing then that she had discussed the matter after all, Mother would become shy, just like a young girl. Then, to avoid being put on the spot, she would cut across the room, go into the hall, slip on wooden clogs, and go out to the yard, acting for all the world as if she had just recalled some chore. And in a short while I would hear her carefree laughter coming from the garden and the lightness in her voice as she chatted with someone. An hour or two later she would reappear in my room intent upon the very same discussion.

At one time it seemed to my family that Mother must be intensely interested in the story that she repeated over and over and, thus, if the cause could be removed she might be distracted. Reasoning in this vein, we conspired accordingly. When Mother focused on sending a gift to so-and-so, my wife, Mitsu, would show her the article, wrap it in her presence, and give it to our housekeeper with instructions to take it to the post office. But Mother was not to be out-witted by such maneuvers. She would watch suspiciously while Mitsu wrapped the package and say spiteful things such as, "Even if you do that, I can't be sure you'll really send it." Disagreeable as such behavior was, there was something reassuring about it, for it revealed that a part of her was perceptive enough to discern hidden strategies. And if for the moment she appeared to be deliberately perverse in repeating her spiteful allegations, if her behav-ior appeared rebellious to everyone, we soon learned that Mother was not being either rebellious or spiteful. After an hour or so, she had no recollection whatsoever of Mitsu wrapping the package in her presence, nor of anything else that had happened.

However, the scratched record in Mother's head rarely played the same words for any length of time. For some reason the resident who had inhabited her mind and oc-cupied her complete attention would suddenly depart and a new resident would appear. Even Soko, who knew Mother best, had no idea why the old one suddenly disap-peared. What is more, once Mother stopped talking about a subject, we could not get her to return to it even if we wanted to. She became totally indifferent to it. Nor was there any way of knowing why the new resident moved in. The content of Mother's repeated conversations was varied. Mostly, though, there were her wishes for things to be done for her, there were reports of information she had heard from others, and there were reminiscences of experiences in the distant past. It never became clear why these particular things should so often jog her consciousness.

It was late one evening last summer when I became aware that Mother frequently brought up the name of Shunma, a male relative who died at the age of seventeen in 1893 or 1894. I had invited a guest to a restaurant in Tsukiji in downtown Tokyo, and it was after eleven o'clock when I returned home. As I relaxed on the living room couch, I heard Mother's voice mingled with the voices of my children in the adjacent room. I remarked to Mitsu, "Granny's here, isn't she?" (My family, my sisters, brother, and I all called her "Granny.")

"Yes, she is. But I don't know why she came," Mitsu replied, laughing. She explained that toward evening Soko had called to say that, quite uncharacteristically, Mother had announced her desire to come to our house. "I'm sure she'll want to come right home again after an overnight stay, but once she sets her mind on something she won't budge. I'm sending her over by taxi, so please take care of her."

"Granny, I can tell that you loved Shunma, but it's not proper for you to keep saying Shunma this, Shunma that. At your age—eighty—you shouldn't talk like that." There was emphasis on the "shouldn't." "You just shouldn't." It was my second son, a third-year high school student, speaking.

"No, I did not love him," Mother said.

"Ah, Granny, you're copping out. Granny, you did love Grandpa Shunma, didn't you? Eh, did you dislike him? Tell me, you didn't dislike him, did you?"

"Why are you calling him Grandpa Shunma? He was not an old man at all. He was just about your age."

"If he were alive, he'd be about ninety now, wouldn't he?"

"I wonder about that. I don't think he'd be that old."

"But wasn't he seven or eight years older than you, Granny?"

"You say, 'if he were alive today . . . ,' but he died at that time, so he can't be. He was just about your age. But even if the ages are similar, he was much nicer and much more intelligent than you."

Mother's voice was drowned in the children's laughter. It sounded as if someone fell backward for the sliding door rattled. My second son had been speaking, but I could hear the laughter of my elder son, a university student, and of my younger daughter, a middle school student. Mingled with the children's laughter I could discern Mother's laugh, for she was apparently going along with them. They were extremely gay.

"We shouldn't let the children tease Granny," I said.

"It's really Granny's fault," Mitsu replied. "Whenever she comes here, she corners the children and talks to them only of Shunma."

"What does she say?"

"Oh, such things as 'Shunma was very kind.' 'He was an outstanding student who entered the First Higher School at seventeen.' 'Had he lived he would probably have been a great scholar.' With such talk no wonder the children want to tease her. She also brags in the same vein about his younger brother, Takenori, but she doesn't seem to do it as much. Remember, we recently invited Granny over for dinner on the anniversary of Grandpa's death. All she did then was talk about Shunma. So I told her not to talk so much about Shunma and asked her to talk a little bit about Grandpa or it wouldn't be right for Grandpa."

I had not known at all that Mother talked like that. My wife's expression showed that she thought it strange I hadn't known. "It's been some time since she started talking about Shunma. You haven't heard her talk about him? I wonder . . . maybe she won't talk about him in your presence because you are her son. Granny certainly must have loved him a lot."

"I'm astonished. Father's left out in the cold, isn't he?" I remarked.

I also had some recollection of the names of Shunma and his brother Takenori. They were members of a family that was related to our family. In other words, they were Mother's cousins once removed; and Mother's father, my grandfather, and Shunma and Takenori were cousins. These brothers had lost both parents early in life and were taken in by Mother's family to be raised with her. But Shunma had died shortly after he entered the First Higher School, and Takenori also died while attending the same school, both at the age of seventeen. Since they had qualified to enter the First Higher School at that age, they were probably outstanding students, just as Mother said. In the family plot in our village, the gravestones of these two youths rest side by side in the southeast corner; the older brother carries our surname, while the younger brother's surname is unchanged. Ever since I was very young I had felt as if some trespassers were resting in our family plot.

After learning about Mother's incessant chatter about Shunma, I began to pay more attention unconsciously. I realized I was the only one in the house who had not known about it: even our housekeeper knew that Mother talked about Shunma as if he were her sweetheart. When I told this to Soko, she said, "Granny never talks about him in my presence, but it's well known even to our relatives in the village. I wonder if it might be out of reserve on her part that she doesn't discuss it in front of us, her children. Granny's still able to exercise some discretion, isn't she?"

What Mother had to say about Shunma was really very uncomplicated. He was a gentle youth; he was an outstanding student; and one day when he was studying and she approached the veranda from the garden, he asked her to join him. That was all. Mother must have been seven or eight at the time. This invitation was something the young girl who was to become my mother would remember all her life. Mother revealed no more than that. It seemed that it was not a matter of not wanting to say more, just that there was nothing more to say. Of all the things that interested her, Shunma alone held her continued attention no matter how much time passed. In this way, he was different from the other residents in her mind.

This matter was often the subject of talks between my sisters, brother, and me whenever we got together. We all agreed that when Mother was a young girl she must have loved that brilliant boy who died so young. We could come to no other conclusion. Since the older brother had even changed his surname, he might have been betrothed to her. And whenever we talked like this, someone was certain to say that even if this was so, it was embarrassing to have her talk so excessively of Shunma and forget about Father, who had been her husband for a lifetime. This talk always ended with laughter, for here was a distinctly comical aspect, as well as an unexpected dimension, in our mother, and we experienced something that was neither quite shock nor betrayal in having all this revealed to us at so late a date.

We were old enough not to feel disgust at learning that Mother had felt the stirring of love at an early age and cherished it throughout her life. We knew that even Father, in his grave, would not feel particularly strongly about it had he known. "Oh, is that so?" is probably all he would have said. In any case, it had happened over seventy years ago, and even though my family and I said such things as "hopeless Granny," we felt somehow refreshed, as if cooled by a breeze.

I expressly forbade my children to tease their grandmother, but whenever she came over, Granny herself would start things by telling them, as though for the first time, how Shunma did such-and-such. At first the children paid no attention and affected boredom, but she kept on and they ended by teasing her. Whenever she began talking about Shunma, a certain shyness came over her, and a manner that suggested "I really shouldn't talk about it, but, well, maybe I'll just tell them a little." Since Mother always forgot that she had already talked about him so much to her grandchildren, whenever she started on the subject her manner had all the charm of innocence, which to this day remains unforgettable.

I took to observing her face as she talked, the way one would watch the antennae of an insect. (Naturally, since Mother never talked about him to me, I had to glance in her direction when she talked to the children.) I perceived not a trace of boldness, but rather, in addition to hesitation and reticence, a certain brooding expression on her face when she dwelt on this topic. As I watched, I could not help being moved. How that young girl must have loved that boy! I thought. For in her worn words and her worn expression was a pathos quite apart from anything attributable to mere age. And in the light laughter that is unique to the aged and the serenity that I saw on these rare occasions, there was something that told me I should stand back and watch silently.

"That saying—that it's all right to have children with women but they can't be trusted—it's true, isn't it?" I once remarked to my wife.

"I wonder if that's the way it is. Perhaps Granny is a special case." As Mitsu replied, she eyed me as if she were searching my soul. Seeing Granny like this, Mitsu reflected, made her think life was purposeless. But I feel

32

that whether a person's life has been purposeful or not depends on one's viewpoint: one could say there is little meaning in the physical love between a couple who live out their lives together; but if an emotional love—even just a tiny fragment—has endured throughout a person's life, then one cannot say that life has been entirely wasted. From either viewpoint there is pathos, just as there was pathos in Mother's face. There was also some sadness in my discussion with Mitsu. It seems inevitable that when judging a person's life at its conclusion, there are some aspects that make one pessimistic about the purpose of existence. At any rate, I can belïeve this as I see Mother today and understand that what I see is the conclusion of life for one who has lived eight decades.

Last summer Mitsu's mother died in Hiroshima. It happened in the house of her second daughter, that is, the home into which Mitsu's younger sister had married. On my side of the family we are long-lived, and the same goes for my wife's side. Mitsu's father died toward the end of the war at the same age as my father—eighty—and her mother passed away at the age of eighty-four. At the beginning of last summer news arrived that Mitsu's mother's condition had taken a turn for the worse, and my wife left immediately for Hiroshima, where she nursed her mother for about half a month and was with her at her deathbed. I had a cold and could not attend the funeral. My visit at the end of May was the last time I saw my mother-in-law.

Mitsu stayed on at her sister's house for two weeks after the funeral. This was unusual, for Mitsu dislikes being away from her own home, but there were things to clear up afterward and Mitsu seemed to feel that, with her mother gone, this might be the last time she would spend so many days under the same roof as her sister. At dinner on the day of Mitsu's return, she talked about her mother's death. She talked of things she had seen and of things she had heard from her sister. "All grannies are alike, aren't they?" she remarked, as she told us about her mother.

A month before my mother-in-law died, she began to call out incessantly for her elder sister, who had been her sur-rogate mother. "Sister, give me some hot water!" "Sister, get me my medicine!" She called upon her sister to perform all these chores.

She had been sick in bed for almost a year, but up to the last month she had been almost more clearheaded than anyone around her. Every morning she would ask for fresh water to be placed on the family altar, where her deceased husband's mortuary tablet reposed, and at times from her bed she wrote letters of thanks to people who had visited her. "Grandpa did this, Grandpa did that," she would say, and not a day passed without mention of her husband, who had died ten years ago.

Then it suddenly stopped, and she never mentioned his name again but began calling for her sister. The way she called her—much as a younger child might wheedle an older sister—coming from the mouth of an eighty-four-year-old woman, sounded grotesque.

34

"When I was there, she also mistook *me* for her elder sister. 'Sister! You've come to visit me!'" my wife imitated.

"Ugh, that sounds weird," said my elder son.

"Strangely enough, it wasn't a bit repulsive. I was amazed how a child's voice could come from such an old person. It was soft and babyish. It even surprised the nurse, who said, 'She's starting to call for her sister again.' And from that time she gradually regressed and became more of a child so that two or three days before she died she finally became an infant. She sucked her thumb noisily. She probably thought it was a breast. It was just like an infant."

I could not imagine my eighty-four-year-old mother-in-law sucking her thumb. But since I'm told that her body gradually shriveled as she approached death, I suppose if I had seen her after she became so small such behavior may not have appeared unnatural.

"After seeing our Hiroshima Granny," Mitsu said to me, "I think I can now understand Granny. I think that Granny is also walking back toward her infancy. Right now she's stopped at about ten years of age. I don't think I'm mistaken about this. It's not that she can't forget Shunma; it's that she has returned to the age when she used to play with him."

I could not contradict Mitsu's views and had to agree.

"Of course, Granny is ten years old," our younger daughter said. "That means she's at an age before she married Grandpa, and it's natural that she wouldn't know anything about him. It's because she hasn't met Grandpa yet."

"Our Hiroshima Granny had a faster tempo," my

younger son added. "She regressed to a young girl, then a child, then an infant, and then she died. Granny is still healthy and so she'll stay at ten for many more years. We'll be hearing about Shunma for some time yet."

Our elder son spoke next. "In other words, to grow younger—rather than older—means that the past disappears. It would be interesting if the regression is total, but it's hard when there are parts that are not erased. The inconvenient parts disappear and the other parts remain. In poor Granny's case, it seems she's been blamed unjustly quite a bit."

As I listened to my family I wondered whether they were correct in applying Mitsu's mother's case directly to that of my own mother, and yet I also believed that as people age this might well be true and Mother was probably no exception. Certain parts of her past had completely disappeared. She had definitely forgotten about Father, and her interest in her own children had declined to such an extent that it could not be compared with what it once had been. It was hard to tell whether she felt any love for her grandchildren at all. Looked at this way, Mother might be likened to an eraser, rubbing off from one end the long line of life she had drawn. Naturally, it was not something Mother was conscious of; old age had its grip on this eraser. It was an inevitable process and old age was inexorably wiping off the line of life closest to the present.

Father, I believe, did not erase anything up to the time of his death. The line he walked was drawn clearly, with a thick, firm stroke. He did not regress to age ten, much less to infancy. Rather, I think that it was as a father that he had held his child's hand, my hand, as he neared the end of his eighty years of life. But perhaps in his final moments old age had got hold of the eraser surreptitiously. I could not be certain that this did not happen.

After this conversation, I talked about Mother as a ten-year-old with my sisters and brother.

"Then Granny, too, might suck her thumb in the future. Oh, how cute she'll look when she gets like that," said Soko. "But meanwhile, you know what her latest preoccupation is? It's funeral gifts of money. Whenever she hears of a death in our village, she makes a big fuss about sending a gift. Until she's convinced we've sent it, she nags such a lot I can't stand it. She has the old record of past funeral gifts—so much from so-and-so, so much from so-and-so —but you know how times have changed. There are some families to whom we don't have to send anything now, but she can't understand that. And also, as you know, the value of money has changed. She can't understand that, either. I definitely don't agree that she's ten."

When Soko, who lived with Mother and knew her daily activities best, said this about funeral gifts, my brother and I were persuaded she was right. "When Granny's talking about funeral gifts, she's every inch a strong-willed old woman," said my sister. "Death equals funeral gifts, doesn't it? And when she hears somebody has died, she reacts immediately with the idea that she has to return the gift. She acts as if she's borrowed money."

∾

This spring I planned a flower-viewing trip for my immediate family and those among my brother's and sisters' families who were able to participate, as a kind of informal entertainment for Mother in celebration of her eightieth birthday. We were to travel through Shimoda, where we would stay overnight at the newly built Kanagawa Hotel, then drive past Amagi and stop at our village in Izu. There our schedule entailed a visit to Father's grave. Who were going was decided upon well in advance, and hotel reservations were made early in January, but we kept all this from Mother. Soko requested that Mother be kept in the dark until just before the trip because otherwise she would talk of nothing else, repeating the same question day after day, "Tell me, when are we going?" This would drive everyone around her to distraction. For that reason we decided not to let Mother know until the day before we were to leave.

But early in April, somehow, Mother found out she was to accompany us to Izu on a flower-viewing trip, and several days before our departure she started telephoning my house morning and night. Soko was in her beauty shop every day, and Mother would slip in her calls during her absence. Mother seemed particularly anxious about whether or not she could visit the village. When whoever took the call assured her that we would definitely stop there, she would say, "Oh! that's wonderful!" each time, then promptly forget the conversation.

There was great confusion when we did leave. Soko and Mother stayed the night with us in order to allay Mother's suspicion that she would be left behind.

38

On the appointed day we piled into two cars and set out for Tokyo Station. But no sooner had we got around the corner when Mother exclaimed, "Oh! I forgot something important. But it can't be helped. It's all right." When we asked her what she had forgotten, it turned out to be her handbag. Soko, sitting in front by the driver, denied this because she herself had given Mother the handbag at the front door. We stopped the car and everyone got out to search, but the handbag was nowhere to be found. I had the car return to the house. There, on the azalea bush beside the entrance, was Mother's handbag, with a handkerchief folded into a neat square and a piece of paper on it. We could not understand why Mother had left it there.

My brother, sister-in-law, and their two children were waiting for us at Tokyo Station. Because of other commitments, my other sister, who comes immediately after me in order of birth, and her husband could not join us. However, their high-school-aged daughter and their eldest son, who had graduated from college the previous year and was now employed by a brokerage firm, were coming. The fact that Mother did not see these two grandchildren right away seemed to worry her. While I was giving our luggage to the porters, Mother looked about her distractedly and, possibly seeing figures resembling her grandchildren among the crowds in the station, would suddenly start to wander away. I instructed my two sons to look after her. Meanwhile, as time passed and her two grandchildren failed to appear, Mother became pale with worry.

"We still have thirty minutes before the train leaves.

They'll make it in time," my second son assured her.

"My handbag!" Mother suddenly screeched. When all heads turned toward her, she also looked around.

"I have it," my younger daughter said.

"You shouldn't do that," my elder son rebuked. "If you're holding it, you should let us know so we won't worry."

"That's all right. That's all right. I'll hold it," Mother said.

"Granny, you can't," someone said.

Eventually the two grandchildren arrived and the whole group moved toward the platform, Mother stopping from time to time to fuss when she thought someone was missing. Each time she was scolded by a grandchild, she responded with a merry little embarrassed laugh.

After we boarded the Ito-bound train and it started to move, Mother, who up till then had been fussing constantly over others, became quiet. She composed herself, sitting primly in Japanese fashion, with her hands in her lap, and gazed out the window. As if this were the proper etiquette for train travel, Mother behaved with the utmost decorum as she took in the view along the line. From a short distance away I observed her face turned toward the window and noted that, in contrast to her harried involvement before boarding, she was now totally alone. The impression she projected was that of a solitary old woman traveling by herself.

At the Kanagawa Hotel we settled into our rooms on the side that faced the sea and overlooked an expansive lawn.

We could not have asked for more on a flower-viewing trip, for we had hit upon the very day the cherry blossoms were at their best. Through the windows we could see masses of blossoms everywhere, as solid and unmoving as artificial flowers smudged on a canvas with great daubs of color. We could not see the sea from our rooms, but the breeze brought us the sound of the waves.

We split up into groups and strolled about the huge lawn before dinner. After we had arrived at the hotel Mother expressed her dissatisfaction each time she spoke. She may have thought, "This place is not Izu. Izu is certainly not like this." At any rate, to the women, who all exclaimed to her, "Isn't it beautiful!" she seemed to reply by her attitude, "No matter how many times you repeat the word beautiful, I don't have to agree blindly." At such times Mother looked slightly rebellious, like a petulant child, a ten-year-old girl; yet at the same time she looked her age, an old woman of eighty.

At about seven we dined together in the large dining room, where several tables were pushed together in a corner and adults and children sat wherever they liked. Only Mother had a special place—at the center of the group. She might have been tired, for she had only soup, hardly touched the rest of the food, and was rather quiet. But she was full of smiles. Unlike our deceased father, she seemed pleased that all these people had gathered for her sake.

After dinner we returned to our rooms, then almost everyone immediately went outside. My brother and I withdrew to the room we shared and talked the way brothers do when they meet after a long time. During the day, our room had been a busy scene of people coming and going, but now it was different. The rooms on either side of us were quiet. My brother remarked that it looked as though everyone was out viewing the cherry blossoms. At that, I joined him at the window and looked out. Below I could see the women and children from our party, split up into two or three groups, cutting across an expanse of lawn that was artificially lit up. The cherry trees next to the hotel were illuminated and appeared to float, as in a stage setting, while the trees at the other end of the lawn were engulfed in darkness. There had been talk in the dining room that the blossoms seen in darkness were the most spectacular, and the women and children seemed to be veering in that direction.

After a while my brother went down to the reception desk. Since his wife was leaving our group the following day to return to Tokyo, I surmised that he had gone to take care of her train reservations. After he left, I heard a small sound come from next door. There shouldn't be anyone there, but it suddenly occurred to me that Mother might have remained behind in the room. I recalled that I hadn't seen her when I looked out the window a short time before.

I quickly stepped into the hall and tried the door to the adjacent room, which was shared by Mother and Soko. It opened right away, and as I entered I could see Mother seated Japanese-style on the bed farthest from the window. She had assumed the same posture as in the train, prim and straight-backed, with her hands in her lap.

"Shu-chan came to ask me to go out a while ago, but I wanted to rest."

She said this in a manner that suggested she was almost self-conscious at being discovered alone in the room. The Shu-chan she referred to is my elder son. I decided to keep her company for a while, and as I sank into a chair near the window my attention was drawn to the handbag lying on the table. I picked it up and looked inside. It contained a slightly dog-eared notebook, nothing else. I said, "There's nothing in here, is there?"

"There is. If not, then Soko must have put all the things in her bag." So saying, she started to get off the bed, as though agitated by my remark, but when I stopped her, she remained where she was.

I removed the notebook from her handbag and opened it. It was the funeral gift record. There, on one page, in Father's handwriting, was the list of names of families and stores, and on the opposite page the various sums of money given. The earliest date on the first page was 1930. Startled at coming across this in such a place, I stared at Mother.

"Why did you bring the funeral gift ledger?" I asked.

"Oh, is that in there? I must have brought it without knowing." She looked as embarrassed as a child questioned about some mischief, and once again she started to get down from the bed to retrieve the ledger. I brought the handbag to Mother and returned to my seat by the window.

"It's strange . . . I don't know anything about it. I wonder if Soko put it here." So saying, Mother tilted her head like someone intensely puzzled. It was not likely that Soko would put this sort of thing in her bag. Mother must have put it there herself, and she must have done so knowingly.

At this point my brother entered the room.

"There seem to be a lot of guests here, but all the rooms are empty. They must all have gone outside," he said, sitting down across from me.

"By the way, what's our schedule for tomorrow? Where are we going from here?" Mother asked, as she tried to hide the handbag behind her. She looked as if it would be terrible if the discussion of the ledger should come up again in my brother's presence. Even though her question had already been discussed several times, I went over our schedule for the following day again. I added that we would visit Father's grave in the village, but that it would probably be too much for her to climb the hill to the cemetery.

"Yes, I think I will beg off visiting the grave. It's slippery on that hill. And besides, I'd like to be released from my duties toward Grandpa from now on. I did all kinds of things for him. I can stop now, can't I?"

Mother smoothed the sheet on the bed as she spoke, her eyes on her hands. She had abandoned her usual manner of speaking and uttered these words seriously and with deep feeling. As I watched, I felt I was witnessing something very strange. Mother seemed to have leaped from her ten-year-old world to sensible adulthood. And it was unusual for her to talk about Father. Then she raised her head and gazed beyond us into space, deep in thought. "Once I went to meet him when it was snowing. I went with the lady next door. The road was frozen," she said suddenly.

From her tone and expression it was obvious that Mother was in the midst of one of her reminiscences. It was as if she meant to address my brother and me, but her tone made it seem she was talking to herself. She was probably recalling a journey to meet Father somewhere. In the past Mother had spent some time in the area called "the snow country." She gave birth to me at Asahigawa, where a division headquarters was located, and a division had been stationed at Hirosaki, too, the last post, where Father had received his retirement papers. She had also lived for two years in Kanazawa. It was undoubtedly in one of those northern cities that she had gone to meet Father, but it wasn't clear which one. Then Mother continued in the same tone, "Shu-chan seems to take his own lunch to school. Well, I also made lunch every day. I really had a hard time making dishes to go with the rice."

My brother and I listened silently. Something told us not to interrupt.

"I polished his boots, too. There are so many places to polish on military boots," she continued.

It seemed an X-ray had just penetrated a part of Mother's mind, a keen arrow of light piercing the inside of her head making a slice of memory become crystal clear. And Mother was pulling that out and expressing it in words. Ordinarily she didn't consciously try to remember things; the things she did recall emerged spontaneously. But this was different. Now she was drawing from her memory fragments of the hardships she had suffered because of Father. Her voice was tinged with resentment.

When Mother fell silent, my brother said, "Granny, when we lived in Hirosaki, we did go to the castle for flower-viewing, didn't we?"

My brother seemed aware that Mother was remembering only painful episodes from her life with Father, and he was trying to help her recall some bright, happy times. But Mother would not be distracted.

"Oh," she said, "did we?"

She looked at us, and the tension in her face of a moment ago, when she was concentrating with all her might on wrenching out the past, vanished.

"There was a garden party at Eiju Hospital in Kanazawa, wasn't there?" my brother asked. Mother's expression did not change.

"Remember? All the families of military doctors got together and it was very merry."

"Was that so?"

"You won second place in the lottery."

"No, I don't remember any of it." Mother shook her head decisively. She truly did not seem to remember.

"Then do you remember these things?" Now, with mounting agitation, my brother recalled various incidents from the distant past which Mother undoubtedly had enjoyed. She had forgotten almost all of them, and of the few she remembered she seemed to retain only vague impressions.

In time she seemed to become annoyed at my brother's

questions, and also somewhat embarrassed at her own almost total lack of recall.

"Well, I think I'll go to sleep now," she said presently, and with that she lay down. It was a good time to leave.

As my brother and I were going out, he said, "Let's go to the garden, too," and I agreed. In the corner of the large garden by the hotel we saw the shadowy figures of several groups of hotel guests and young couples. Our party must be around somewhere, but it was hard to make them out. The human figures on the illuminated lawn looked small and stiff.

The night air was neither hot nor cold, and the gentle breeze that caressed my cheeks bore the salty scent of the sea. My brother and I entered the lighted area and cut across the wide lawn toward a row of cherry trees some distance away on our right.

"Mother has forgotten all the happy times in her life with Father and remembers only the painful events. Old people seem to share this tendency, don't you think?" my brother said. His voice was somewhat tense, reacting to what he had just observed in Mother. He must have brooded about it since we left her room. "When you look at a pillar in an old temple, the soft portion of the wood wears away and becomes recessed with the years and only the hard portion remains. It's similar with the aged. The good memories disappear and the bad ones remain."

One could indeed look at it that way, I thought. In those unusually lucid moments Mother had dragged forth from the pit of her memory those incidents of hardship—going

47

to meet Father in the snow, making his lunches, and polishing his boots—to justify her wish not to visit his grave any more.

However, my own thoughts differed slightly from my brother's, for I, too, had been dwelling on what we had witnessed. If Mother had forgotten all her happiest memories, she had, in a similar way, lost all her most painful memories. She had forgotten how she had been loved by Father and how she had loved him; she had also forgotten how she had been ill-treated by him, as well as how cold she had been toward him at times. In this sense, the ledger of their life together was well balanced. Her recollections tonight of going to meet Father, polishing his boots, and making his lunches were probably not considered as hardships when she was doing them, when she was young. However, now in her old age these trivialities, accumulated like dust over a long period of time, must weigh on her more heavily. In the simple process of living, such dust settles daily on a person's shoulders, almost imperceptibly. Was not Mother simply feeling its weight?

I put off revealing these thoughts to my brother. Soon we arrived at the cherry trees. The myriad clusters of small, full blossoms spread over our heads like an umbrella. The strong light did not reach this area. A single nearby torch cast a dim half-light, and within that dimness the blossoms shone with a lavender cast. Just then, another idea caught up with me, pursuing my thoughts of a moment before. Perhaps that dust only gathers on a woman's shoulders. Perhaps during a long conjugal life, out of some process totally unrelated to love or hate, it is something a husband thrusts on his wife, that day-to-day accretion of resentments that are not really resentments. If that is so, then the husband is the persecutor and his wife the victim.

Pressed by my brother, I set these thoughts aside and we left the trees to return to the hotel. Now the lights in all the rooms were on. Mother was in one of those distant, brightly lit rooms. She had been lying down when we left, but she would be sitting up primly now. There was no way that I could understand the structure of my aged mother's mind, but somehow I knew—both of us knew, although my brother did not say anything—that Mother was sitting on the bed.

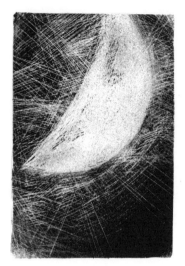

The Light
of
the Moon

When Mother reached eighty, I decided I would write about her aging. This I did in "Under the Blossoms," in a form that was neither a novel nor an essay. Five years have elapsed since then and Mother will be eighty-five this year. She has already lived five years longer than Father, and since Father died in 1959, this also means that Mother has lived as a widow for ten years.

The eighty-five-year-old Mother of today should appear much older than the eighty-year-old Mother of "Under the Blossoms," but this is not so at all. It is true that she seems to have grown smaller, but her sight has not deteriorated, her hearing is no worse, and her stamina seems unchanged. The skin on her face is lustrous and appears even more youthful than before, and there is no hint of the ugliness of old age, no trace of meanness in her bright smile. In her activities, such as running over to see the neighbors several times a day, she seems to have forgotten to add to her years. She does not complain of stiff shoulders and she seldom catches cold. She has lost only a few of her molars, and those long ago. Indeed, if I had to point out any change in her in the past few years it would be her two false front teeth. Mother will never know the discomfort of wearing a full set of dentures in her life.

As in the matter of her teeth, so with her eyesight. She can still read the small print of newspaper captions without glasses—which she does aloud, as though reading to herself—something none of her four children can match. Whenever the four of us discuss Mother, one of the first things mentioned, usually with a sigh, is "Granny's in the

53

best of health, isn't she?" or "Granny's certainly strong."

"I wonder if Granny ever had stiff shoulders in her forties and fifties?" Soko once remarked, when she herself was of an age when she might expect such symptoms. But no one could answer immediately. One of us said, "Well, Mom must have had something like that in her late forties," to which another remarked dejectedly, "Well, if that were the case, then she would be like other people." In truth, the only person who could have enlightened us on that subject was Father, for he alone was with her during that period—in other words, during the late 1920s when he retired from the army and withdrew to Izu, when the two of them were at the threshold of their older years and we children were setting up our own homes in the city. But Father was dead. We always concluded such speculations with the observation that children really do not know much about their mothers, that we were all ignorant of the period in our mother's life when she was stepping into old age, the threshold all of us had already crossed or were about to cross.

Mother has always been small, but around the time of Father's death her flesh began to shrink and she became even tinier. Now her shoulders and chest are so slight that one sometimes wonders if this can possibly be a human frame. If one were to pick her up, would her weight be only composed of bones? As I observe her movements, I am reminded of the lightness of a withered leaf. I also feel the tenuousness of life—that from here her body has no other place to go to than its ultimate end.

Two years ago I had a dream about Mother. I don't know where it took place, but it seemed to be in the street in front of our house in the village. Mother was standing there waving her arms, desperately resisting being blown away by the wind, shouting, "Please, someone, hurry and save me!" After I had that dream I became aware that in reality Mother's movements had a strangely buoyant and airy quality, suggesting that she might well be caught up by a strong gust of wind and carried away somewhere. Since then I have become more aware of the fragile lightness of her body.

When I mentioned this once to my sister Shikako, however, her response was, "It would be simple if Granny were just frail."

"You try it for a week," she went on. "No, three days would be enough. Try living with Granny for three days. Then you wouldn't have the luxury of thinking about her frailty. Seriously, I'm at my wit's end to know what to do. I feel at a loss, then I get sad; and sometimes I reach the point where I want to die with her."

When my sister said this, we all had to agree with her, and I regretted having thoughtlessly brought up my view as a mere onlooker. I quickly changed the subject so as not to further agitate Shikako.

Mother is currently living in the Izu house in the care of Shikako and her husband, who works at the town hall. Shikako, representing the four of us, is looking after Mother alone in her old age. To Shikako it is only natural for the daughter to look after her own mother, but even so, in her present situation as the one who has the physical care of our mother, she must feel she has a hard lot.

Shikako took over Soko's role of a few years ago. The single change that has taken place within the past several years in Mother's living arrangements is that she has moved from Soko's place in Tokyo to Shikako's home in the Izu village. Mother has been placed in the care of her elder instead of her younger daughter.

I have described in "Under the Blossoms" how we children decided, after Father died, that we could not leave our aged mother to live alone in the home village; how after much fussing on Mother's part it was arranged that Soko would undertake her care, and how Mother reluctantly agreed to come to Tokyo as she would be looked after by her own daughter. Mother has always been nervous in my house or my brother's, although I feel one of her sons should rightfully have assumed the responsibility. She seems to feel that even if she has to accept help from her daughters, she will not live in a son's home, where strangers have entered the family. She has repeatedly said, "I have done as I pleased all my life, and at my age I certainly don't intend to live with my sons and feel ill at ease and inhibited even in such matters as what I eat."

Mother lived with Soko for about four years. Her senility became noticeably more pronounced after being in Tokyo for two or three years, when she was about seventy-eight or seventy-nine, although the earliest traces were already apparent before Father's death. In retrospect, there were various symptoms that revealed that part of Mother's brain might be damaged, but no one noticed because her aggressiveness had also became more marked.

We first became aware of the severity of her condition when we realized that Mother herself did not understand, or accept, the fact that she kept forgetting what she said and repeated herself.

"Granny, you've already said that many times."

When someone brought that to her attention, it did not serve any purpose. Mother never believed it, and even in her docile moods she would merely return a dubious look and that was about the extent of it. Moreover, although she heard what was said, she retained it only that moment and promptly forgot about it. It made us feel as if our words only scuffed her mind momentarily but left no trace. Mother tended to repeat herself in the same way that a scratched record does. At first we interpreted her repetitiveness as an obsession with certain topics, but we later changed our minds. True, if something stimulated her mind in a special way and thus became engraved on the record, it would play automatically and persistently for a certain period of time. But no one could divine the circumstances in the intervening period when certain things would be selected, nor the reasons they became engraved in her mind. At times certain things would be repeated for days, and then—for some unknown reason—she would suddenly stop. All one could conclude was that what had been engraved had suddenly disappeared. Sometimes this would happen after one or two hours; at other times it would persist for ten or twenty days.

57

The topics Mother repeated in this manner were not only the results of recent stimulation but also of old memories that had been engraved decades ago in the distant past. From memories of her youth, for example, only certain episodes chose to appear although no one knew why they were special. In any case only very few of them were special. These seemed to have been indelibly imprinted on her memory, never appearing with any urgency but seeming to be waiting their turn, emerging at times that did not appear too illogical. In such situations Mother acted as though she had just remembered them that moment, and she talked in a way that suggested she was pulling her memories out one at a time from the dim past, with a faraway look in her eyes. There was a spontaneity in that behavior, and undoubtedly each time she thought she was recalling them for the first time. Those who had already heard them before were thoroughly bored, but a first-time listener detected nothing strange. It was only when she repeated the topic after a few minutes' interval, as though she were bringing it up fresh, that you realized her abnormality.

In receiving guests she betrayed no trace of her problem to those who listened for only a short time. She dealt with them correctly from moment to moment, said nothing out of order, and the social ease she had commanded since her youth expressed itself in her quiet agreement with the other person's words and in her special way of establishing a sense of intimacy with others. After talking with her for any length of time, however, one could not help but notice her senility. Mother's words and those of her guests lived only for a moment: the instant they were uttered, she had already forgotten them.

Soko, who lived with our semifunctioning mother from morning to night, naturally reached a point where she could do nothing but lament. Whenever she came to my house she would say, "She's such a good Granny. If only she would stop repeating herself. If I reply, I have to give her the same answer, and if I don't, senile as she is, she gets angry. She must think she's being put down. At such times I just can't stand it. You know, the parts that are broken and the parts that are not are all jumbled together. I'm amazed at some of the spiteful things she comes up with."

Soko further requested that once in a while she would like at least one day in which she was free of Mother. And I could understand her feelings exactly.

To give Soko a break Mother came to stay with me. Since Mother would not agree to come unless there was some plausible reason, my younger brother took on the job of persuading her each time. When she finally made up her mind to come, she was surprisingly cooperative, allowing herself to be sent over by car with enough clothing in her bag to last a week to ten days. Once in the house, however, she invariably appeared unsettled about sleeping in an unfamiliar room, voiced concern about Soko, and became agitated after a single day. Even so, she must have felt she had some obligation and would stay two or three nights; but it was pitiful to observe how her mind raced all the while to Soko's house. When Mother was with us she spent her time in the yard pulling weeds, or cleaning her room, or else bringing tea to guests. She is by nature someone who cannot sit still for a moment and feels uneasy unless she is busy. Wherever she might be in the house, if she heard the doorbell or the telephone ring she would try to answer it immediately even though everyone tried to stop her. When she did pick up the phone and I listened to her responses, she sounded affable and appeared to understand. But as soon as she put down the receiver she had already forgotten the content of the conversation and she would look horribly embarrassed. In the morning, when her head was rested, she remembered messages comparatively well, but in the afternoon she comprehended next to nothing as far as telephone calls were concerned.

When Mother stayed with us her grandchildren would gather around her at night. She was always a bit reserved in the presence of my wife and me, but was happy when surrounded by her grandchildren. Watching them, I could see that grandmother and grandchildren were a highly congenial group.

It was with that group—made up of university, high school, and middle school students—that Mother always brought up the story of Shunma and Takenori, the two brothers who were her relatives, both brilliant students who entered the First Higher School at the age of seventeen and died from tuberculosis or some such illness in their youth. This old record in Mother's head only played when she was in the company of my children, and she never touched on it in front of Soko or me. Several times during the same evening she would talk about the brothers, always in the belief that it was for the first time, even when her grandchildren brought up the subject and would tease her by confusing Shunma with Takenori. I forbade them to do this, but Mother never got angry with them at such times; she would merely correct them or argue with them, and seemed to be enjoying herself. Her grandchildren came to believe that Shunma had been Granny's betrothed when she was young, and I agreed with them to some extent. According to the inscription on the tombstone of the older brother, he had taken our surname, so even if he had not actually been betrothed to her, Mother might have been led to believe she was to marry Shunma. And if I were to fantasize further, it may have been after Shunma's death that Takenori inherited his brother's position. Then, when Takenori also died young, it would be quite natural for Father to be chosen and to take on her family name. At any rate, Mother's broken record had all the indications of a woman placed in such a predicament. As she spoke repeatedly of these brilliant young men, her face took on a strange expression.

Mother seldom spoke about Father. Shortly after his death she had talked of him constantly just like most widows; indeed, it was difficult not to because there were many matters to be discussed that involved him. But when her mental deterioration began to be obvious, she suddenly stopped talking about him. From this behavior, I could only assume that she had either lost the record of Father or perhaps she had not made one at all.

Furthermore, while Mother was living with Soko in

Tokyo, we became aware that she had begun to erase whole decades of her long life. She was in effect doing this backward, erasing first her seventies, then her sixties, then her fifties, and so on. It was not that she never talked about those years. In the mornings, when she was rested, she would bring up comparatively recent events, but in the afternoons she was rarely able to recall anything of them. More and more, when we mentioned something relating to those times, she would tilt her head to one side and say, "Oh, was there such a time?"

At first we thought she might be feigning ignorance, but it became clear that this was not so. Those memories were simply evaporating from her mind as she gradually erased the life she had lived, going ever backward toward the time of her birth. Some parts were completely erased, others partially, and in some places just a few traces remained. Thus, the fact that Mother no longer talked about Father and concentrated exclusively on her younger days became understandable.

What I wrote in "Under the Blossoms" concerns Mother during this period. The summer when Mother was eighty she left Tokyo and returned to her native home. By that time newspapers were beginning to carry articles about the polluted air in Tokyo, traffic near Soko's house had suddenly increased, and no matter how we looked at it Tokyo no longer seemed the right place for Mother. Just about that time, too, Shikako's husband found a job in our Izu village and decided to move there from Mishima. Thus it was only natural that Mother should live with them. Soko was by now worn out from the years of caring for Mother and wished to be released from her charge, while Shikako believed it would do her good to take over looking after Mother in her last years. Mother herself, it goes without saying, preferred to live in the village where she had many friends rather than in Tokyo.

There was a driving rain on the day she was scheduled to leave Tokyo. She had come to stay the night with me before her departure, and arrangements were made for her to leave from my house. Everyone suggested that she delay the trip for a day, but she was adamant. Even so, she was still concerned about Soko's house, and up to the moment she got in the car she kept asking whether the house had been locked up. Soko admonished her for asking, and each time this occurred Mother looked shy and embarrassed, like a young girl, instead of getting angry as was her wont. Probably she did not get angry because of her happiness at going home.

Toward the end of her stay in Tokyo Mother sometimes succumbed to colds or dizzy spells and took to bed for a day or two, which made the family think she was finally yielding to old age. But after she moved back to the village this did not happen any more. Her color improved so much that she looked like a different person, and she bustled about so diligently that she hardly paused for breath. She insisted, in particular, upon participating in ceremonial events such as weddings and funerals, much to the distress of the family, for even though she was repeatedly advised that a woman over eighty should not appear in public, she simply would not listen. Whenever a circular arrived from the neighborhood association, she would run over with it to the neighbor's—she never walked. Apparently the prospect of a piece of business awaiting her attention made her behave that way, and anyhow running probably suited her body rhythm better than walking and felt more exhilarating. After she took off with the circular, someone from the family would have to go to the neighbor's house to learn the contents. All that meant extra work.

Mother was virtually indefatigable, or so it seemed to those around her. When the household gathered in the family room for tea, diminutive Mother would join them and sit nearby, but she always turned her gaze out toward the garden. Then she would remark that a dog had wandered into the garden or that leaves were falling and she would get up. She could not sit still for long. She brought the garden broom and pan to the yard many times a day and would not allow a single fallen leaf to remain there. On wintry days the family tried to keep her indoors, but it was impossible to guard her all day and she always found opportunities to slip out unnoticed. Mother's tiny figure, searching for the dustpan and broom in the corner of the garden where the moss was swollen with ice crystals, looked so very cold, but such incidents probably toughened her, for she never caught colds after she moved in with Shikako.

For about a year after her return to the village, Mother's memory seemed to improve. Around the beginning of the second year, however, it reverted to the same state as it was in Tokyo, and from that time on her condition gradually but steadily deteriorated. She began repeating herself even more frequently. When I visited her, for instance, the first question she invariably asked was whether the train had been crowded. This question would be repeated many times during the course of my stay, and it was both tedious and pathetic to see her inability to shift from the topic. Apparently her deepest concern regarding my trip to see her was whether or not I had been inconvenienced in the train, and since that concern had been engraved on her record it had to be played a certain number of times. It was the same when I had to return to Tokyo: as soon as Mother learned I was leaving, she would engrave something about that on her record, and this got played repeatedly until I actually walked out the front gate. For that reason the family did all it could to keep things from her until the last minute. One result of this was that Mother always believed things in her world happened suddenly. My visits home, my returns to Tokyo, and many other events in her life must have seemed to occur with startling abruptness.

Shikako, who lived with Mother in this state, would complain to us whenever we visited, just as Soko had done in Tokyo. About two years after Shikako took over the care of Mother, we all noticed her extreme fatigue and her loss of weight. It would be easy to attribute her health problems to the change of life, except that it was clearly

Mother who was the cause. Mother trailed after Shikako all day long. When Shikako worked in the kitchen, Mother was there. When Shikako was at the door receiving guests, Mother was also there, like a young child trailing its mother. As long as Mother was nearby Shikako could find no rest; yet when Mother was out of sight Shikako felt compelled to search for her. When Shikako could not find Mother in the house, she had to look in the yard, and since it was a country house surrounded by over half an acre of land, this presented a considerable problem.

There was no lack of household help—in addition to Sadayo, a young girl from our village who had pitched in to look after Mother since her Tokyo days, there was other help in the person of an aunt from the main family who had been widowed the previous year. But what was most trying was the unsettled air about the whole house where no one could ever relax. "Yes, Granny, I've heard that many times already." If Shikako were to say this, it did not matter so much, but let the young servant or aunt or someone other than her own children say such a thing, and Mother became angry. True, the anger was short-lived because she quickly forgot the cause of it, but while it lasted it was intense and unrestrained. Without giving thought to who the other person might be, Mother would utter such things as "There's no one as cruel as you!" or "You're a monstrous person!" These outbursts would keep the whole household apprehensive and on edge. At such times a different aspect of her personality emerged—that of the aged heiress who had been pampered and spoiled from her early years—and I recalled the volatile face that I had seen in my youth, only now it appeared in a slightly altered form. As long as she was not angry or excited her expression was peaceful, especially when she was repeating some of her favored phrases; and when others laughed and she joined them without knowing they were laughing at her, her expression could be described as that of an innocent young girl. Whenever I visited, I saw all these aspects of Mother.

In the first two or three years after her return to the country Mother continued erasing her seventies, her sixties, her fifties, and her forties. This phenomenon was expressed in a clearer form than during her Tokyo years, for now she never brought up her later years or her middle years. We would say various things to jog her memory, hoping to help her regain some recollection of a certain period, but in most cases it was useless. "Oh yes, perhaps such a thing might have happened," Mother would say in a way that suggested she remembered vaguely, but I am convinced that she usually had no recollection.

We got in the habit of saying, "What are we going to do with you, Granny?" Occasionally she would respond to that remark with a laughing "That's true, it's terrible this senility," which would startle us. But even when she spoke thus of senility it did not mean she was acknowledging it. Rather, it was more as though she had grown exasperated at our stupid questions and decided, "You probably want to hear me say this, and it's easy enough for me, so I'll keep saying it." A covert rebellion could be sensed in those extremely compliant words.

Mother had accompanied my surgeon father to Tokyo, Kanazawa, Hirosaki, and Taipei and had lived at each military post for some years, but by this time she had almost completely forgotten about those events and places. Since she never volunteered comment about them, one had to suppose that period of her past had been obliterated. And yet, though very seldom, when we were talking about an incident from a period she had forgotten, she would inject such remarks as, "Oh, yes, now that I think of it, it's true that that happened. My goodness, was that really I who was there? That's impossible. And yet . . . now when was that?"

We could see that Mother was genuinely surprised at such times. It was as if she had suddenly looked over a cliff and instinctively pulled back, for she would then momentarily withdraw into her own thoughts, tilt her head a little, look serious, and appear lost in reverie. But that lasted only a short while before her expression cleared. Either it became too troublesome for her or she simply resigned herself to the fact that she could never recall the incident.

I have said that Mother had lost her past in this way from about her seventies down through her forties, but the parts that were lost were not painted over completely; instead they seemed to be enveloped in a fog. There were parts where the fog was heavy and parts where it was not, and there were some breaks in the fog through which memory penetrated hazily. I thought that the changes in Mother on her return to the village after Tokyo were probably a result of that fog thickening and spreading.

We, her children, interpreted Mother's obliteration of her past as a gradual walking back toward childhood. This viewpoint was initially expounded by my wife after her own mother died at the age of eighty-four. Unlike my mother, Mitsu's mother remained frighteningly clearheaded until the very end, but about half a year before her death she suddenly began to lose her memory, and once this process began she rapidly reverted to a childlike state. The family members became aware of this regression when my mother-in-law began calling out for her older sister —the sister who had been her surrogate mother—in a distinctively petulant tone of voice. And it was said that two or three days before her death she began pursing her lips, as though feeding at the breast, and sucking her thumb.

"They're the same after all, aren't they?" my wife remarked. "My mother returned to infancy almost instantly, while this Granny's tempo is slower, isn't it? I wonder whether it will take her another twenty years before she gets to that stage."

At first I listened to my wife rather dubiously, but after Mother's return to the village I learned that my brother, my sisters, and I all had, without conscious effort, collected some anecdotes about the elderly. Through Mother we had all become, willingly or not, interested in the problem of aging.

There was a time when we would gather together in our Izu family home and exchange anecdotes. My brother told of an eighty-eight-year-old woman in a farm village outside

Numazu who, two or three years before her death, started bouncing balls and wanted to play with the small beanbags that children like. Probably Granny would take up the children's game of pitching stones pretty soon. Soko relayed a story she had heard from a customer at her beauty shop. This, too, concerned an old woman in her eighties who, for two or three years before her death, could not wait to be given her food at mealtimes and would cover her eyes and sob. There were many such tales, most of them concerning old women, but some about old men. One of these I heard from an acquaintance who worked at a magazine. His father had lived to the age of ninety and had completely regressed to a childlike state in the year of his death. One day this old man bundled all his clothes in a kerchief and tried to leave home. When asked by his family where he was going, he replied he was "going home." It seems the old man had married into this family and he was now trying to return to his place of birth in the neighboring village. The entire discussion had a rather chilling effect, making one want to reassess one's own life.

"But they all became children overnight, didn't they?" Shikako remarked. "In Granny's case there are times when I think she's about ten and at other times she seems to be about thirty. For example, when she's talking about Shunma I think she's about ten, but mostly I think she's about thirty. She talks a lot about events in her thirties."

"She talked most about her thirties when she was in Tokyo, too," said Soko. "If she's still the same, then I wonder whether she is going to stop where she is now.

Otherwise, oh, my, it certainly will take her a long time to reach infancy!"

We speculated about arbitrary stopping points and concluded that if she were to return to her twenties, say, and stop there, or if she were to stop at fifteen or sixteen, she probably wouldn't be as difficult to deal with as she was now.

Finally Shikako's husband, Akio, spoke up. His was a unique view, stemming from his daily contact with his mother-in-law. "I'm not sure at what age Granny stopped or will stop, but I think her change is something that cannot be deduced from chronological age alone. Yes, she has certainly changed in the past year. She has become totally unconcerned about what's going on in the world. One could say that she can no longer distinguish one person from another and leave it at that, but there's more—she no longer shows any interest in visitors to the house. She was not like that previously. Before, when she met a young woman, she always inquired about her marital status, regardless of who the woman might be. With married women, she would ask whether they had any children. She had no other interest in a woman apart from her marital and maternal status. The other thing was her interest in funeral gifts. It's death that she's interested in. Even now, whenever she hears that someone has died she immediately looks for the funeral gift ledger. She shows no sadness over the death but focuses only on the funeral gift."

Reflecting on Akio's words I could see that it was much as he said. It was during the latter part of her stay in Tokyo that she had begun to show a veritable obsession with giving funeral gifts when someone died. This tendency had become more pronounced recently, to the point that she was now positively perfunctory in her attitudes. When she heard that so-and-so was ill she automatically assumed that the person would die, and she went for the funeral gift ledger to check the amount of cash she would have to give, which corresponded to the amount her family had received from that family in the past on a similar occasion. Then, no matter how many times she looked at the ledger, she immediately forgot the sum and had to check it over and over. The figure was meaningless in any case, for the value of money had changed drastically since the old days and she could not compute the difference without help, but she was not satisfied unless she did that.

"I suppose receiving funeral gifts and returning the amount received is definitely the most basic aspect in the give-and-take of human relationships," said Akio. "It's spooky; yet I think it's also beautiful. A person is born, marries, has children, and then dies. If life is condensed, perhaps this is all there is. This has nothing to do with whether Mother has stopped in her thirties or whether she is regressing. Sometimes I wonder what it's all about."

We did not know what to say to Akio. Like it or not, we were all being somewhat protective in the way we viewed Mother, but it seemed it was Akio, her son-in-law, who had got to the heart of the matter, who had most accurately perceived what this particular old woman was doing. After listening to him, I felt I had to reassess my thoughts about Mother's senility. He had said, "I wonder what it's all about." Well, I wondered, too. I had thought of it in terms of something going on in one portion of Mother's mind, like a scratched record that keeps repeating the same refrain, but perhaps there was also something like a small fan spinning around, gradually sifting out for her the extraneous details of her life. After I began to think in this way, Mother's face began to look a bit different to me. I could imagine her reasoning, "Things that are important to me, I will talk about incessantly. It doesn't matter how often I repeat myself, does it? You constantly tell me that I'm forgetful, but naturally I forget trivialities. What is there that I really should remember? Yes, I did go to Taipei, Kanazawa, and Hirosaki, but I didn't enjoy them much. I'll forget all that. I've forgotten about your father, too. Naturally, we had some good times during our marriage. But aren't joy and sadness just transitory moments in this life? There is nothing I would regret forgetting. Why get excited about such insignificant things just because I'm so forgetful? I don't know about men, but the most important events for women are marriage and childbirth. That's why I ask women those things. There is nothing else of importance that I need to ask, is there? Of course I will return funeral money gifts. It is money that we accept in times of tragedy in our family, and this we must return when others are bereaved. They die, we die, and each time this happens we give or receive gifts of money. In the long run we are even—no one loses and no one gains—but such acts are what life is all about. After I die I don't want to be told in

I played a certain role in Uncle Keiichi's return to Japan. Keiichi and his wife Mitsue had no children. Both had taken American citizenship and could live out their lives in the United States if they chose to. However, when I visited their apartment in a New York City suburb during my trip there, Keiichi broached the subject of where to spend the few remaining years of his life, in Japan or America. What did I think? I could not reply with any certainty.

It transpired that Uncle held a rather idealized image of his birthplace, Izu, and since he had lived abroad for over half a century, up to his seventies, and had furthermore become an American citizen, he was a little unsure of life in Japan if he decided to return. As far as I could see, my uncle and aunt's life in New York could only be described as lonely in the extreme, and I thought if they built their own house in Izu they might find some measure of comfort. On the other hand, there was the problem of building a house after arriving in Izu, and they were bound to run into difficulties they could not possibly anticipate while living in an apartment in America. Further, they only had a limited income, so I did not know which would be more advantageous for them financially.

The following year I had occasion to go to America again, so I called on my uncle and aunt in their New York apartment. By that time my uncle had already decided to return to Japan.

" . . . and your mother is still alive," he had said.

I think that Uncle's decision to come home was greatly influenced by the fact that Mother was still well. It seemed that Keiichi, who had returned to Japan only once during his fifty-odd years in America, could not forget his sister as she was the last time he saw her, when she was still young. I warned him that Mother was not the same person she had been then, that she had aged considerably, and had become quite senile.

"Everyone is the same when they age. I'll keep her company. I'm half-senile myself," Uncle responded.

Uncle apparently had prepared a place for his aged sister in his fantasy of life in Japan. Perhaps as a result of his long stay in a foreign land his thinking was rational as well as influenced by Christianity; even his features began to look a little Caucasian.

That fall Uncle and Aunt came to Izu to spend their remaining years. I became their sponsor.

As soon as Uncle got accustomed to the village he built an attractive little Western house and moved in. It was four or five farmhouses beyond Mother's and, with Mother's quick pace, only one or two minutes' away. Every morning, in their small dining room, Uncle and Aunt would make dark toast, meticulously scrape off the burnt surfaces with a knife, and eat it heavily buttered. Since they read the newspapers while they ate, their morning hours were pretty well taken up by breakfast. Neighbors and relatives all called Uncle and Aunt "America-*san*," affixing the Japanese honorific "*san*." There was nothing strange about that as they were both Americans, but it irritated Mother that the person who suddenly appeared before her and claimed to be her brother should be called America-san. It was not her antipathy toward the name itself, but she seemed unable to understand, or accept, the fact that her own brother should be called by such a name.

Until Aunt and Uncle actually returned to Japan, Mother waited with great anticipation. The news that Keiichi was coming home had been engraved on her record and for about half a year it played daily. Keiichi had been Mother's favorite brother from the time she was a young girl. "If only Keiichi were here . . . ," she was often heard to say when there was some incident requiring help. And now that this very Keiichi was coming home, her joy was probably more intense than any of us realized.

Yet when Uncle and Aunt finally did arrive, from the very start Mother did not act particularly pleased, almost as if some part of her had strong doubts whether this was the real Keiichi.

Mother talked and drank tea with Uncle, who visited daily, but she treated him as if he were a new acquaintance who had entered her social circle. She gave no hint that this person could be the brother for whom she had harbored warm feelings all her life and in whom she had wanted to place the utmost trust and confidence whenever something came up.

At first Uncle was gentle with Mother, but her senility was much worse than he had thought, so when she repeated herself excessively he could not avoid reprimanding her some of the time. Even so, the quality of care that a brother shows for a sister is different from that which children feel toward their mother, and whenever Soko or I came to visit, Uncle's attitude was to protect Mother from us.

"Recently Granny doesn't repeat herself very much, does she?" he would inform us. Then he would scold her in a whisper so as to hide her senility from us. This relationship between an aged sister and brother appeared strange to us. Uncle was solicitous of Mother because he genuinely cared a great deal, that was clear, but at other times he became so angry with her that he stalked out with the words, "I'll never come to see such a pig-headed person again!" His chastisement of her was also more severe than any of her children's.

Mother, for her part, stubbornly refused to call him by name. She continually referred to him as "America-san," with a trace of contempt in her tone, and behind his back disparaged him with comments like "Huh, America-san!" or "Who does that America-san think he is!" Despite this, on days he didn't visit she would barge into his house many times, each time forgetting that she had already been there, and return immediately.

"I sometimes wonder whether Granny believes that Uncle Keiichi is really her brother," I would say each time I went to Izu. Even Shikako, who lived with Mother, could not make an accurate assessment. At times she would say, "She does seem to think he's her younger brother Keiichi, after all," at other times, "She just doesn't believe he's her brother." Each time her response was different. In any case, it was apparent to all that in the exchanges between this aged brother and sister, Uncle was getting the short end of the stick. It was as if he had returned to Japan simply to fight with her. He came to visit almost daily, elegant in his neatly pressed trousers, necktie, and sweater. On days when he was not angry with Mother he kept her company, and on days when she irritated him he would not enter the house but walked around the garden and left. At such times Mother often put on her garden clogs and went to join him on his walks. He would refuse to look at her and make as if to leave, but Mother's legs were many times stronger than his and she would either overtake him or beat him home by taking a shortcut. We often observed Uncle and Mother confronting each other in the back yard by the tangerine tree. They looked like bitter adversaries, but at the same time they looked just like an aged sister and brother talking quietly. Judging from my observations of Mother, though, I could only conclude that she regarded him as a challenging companion, nothing more.

One day, at the beginning of summer two years after Uncle returned to Japan, I got an unexpected call from Shikako. It was when Akio had just been released from the hospital following an automobile accident, and he was still on crutches and convalescing at home. Shikako was totally in-censed with Mother. The gist of her call was this.

"I have taken care of Mother for a long time and I am completely worn out. And even if I could still put up with my own fatigue, Mother—for what purpose I'm not sure—continually makes sarcastic and offensive remarks to Akio, who is recuperating at home. This morning she said to him, 'You certainly are fortunate to be able to laze around at home every day.' Even though Akio pays no heed to her comments, it must be unpleasant. We could excuse her by saying that her head is not right and there's nothing we can do about it, but she says these things to him because he's her son-in-law and not her own child. Senile as she may be, she knows that difference. When I got angry with her, she told me it was her home and I could leave. If I could leave I wouldn't suffer so much, but it is precisely because I *can't* leave that I have lost so much weight. I'm afraid I just can't look after Mother any longer. Her senility has got so much worse that I can't take my eyes off her for a second. But setting that aside, Akio needs to go back to the hospital for two weeks for another operation. When that happens, I shall have to commute to the hospital every day, and the problem then becomes what to do about Mother. Mother's not someone who can be managed by Sadayo and Auntie alone. I would like one of you to look after her, at least during Akio's hospitalization."

I had taken the call. Shikako's voice reverberated in the receiver and her extreme agitation came across clearly. That night my brother and Soko came over to discuss what we should do.

"So Granny has finally upset Shikako. I must say, she held up for a long time," Soko remarked.

"She exploded, did she?" my brother remarked. "Naturally, she would. It's hard work, putting up with Mother every day."

We knew Mother might not want to come to Tokyo but we agreed that, whether she did or not, we had to take her there. The situation had changed: Akio was not recovering well from his injuries and we, who had left Mother entirely in the care of Shikako and Akio for years, had to place their interests above all else.

After much discussion it was decided that for the time being Mother would stay with me and then we would take her to Karuizawa, where I have a house which I use for my work during the summer months. We hoped that Mother might find the summer in Karuizawa pleasantly refreshing.

A day or two afterward, Soko and my brother went to Izu to fetch Mother. We had decided to open up the Karuizawa house a little earlier than usual, and our housekeeper and my daughter, Yoshiko, left to prepare the house.

When Mother arrived in Tokyo, accompanied by Soko and my brother, she was so pale and drawn that she looked like a different person. Thinking this was due to her being jostled in the car for four hours, I had her retire early that evening, and Soko and Sadayo, the young girl from the village, slept beside her. But Mother hardly slept at all that night. When she awoke she tried to go downstairs with her luggage, and throughout the night she babbled endlessly about going home.

Toward dawn she finally slept until about ten o'clock. When she came downstairs she looked less fatigued than the previous night and was relaxed enough to praise my garden, saying that it looked lovely.

In the afternoon, however, she was impossible. The

thought that she had to return to the village again invaded her mind, and she trailed Soko around pestering her to leave early or they would not reach home by dusk. Even though we explained the reason she had to come to Tokyo, Mother refused to hear it. It was as if her desire to go home had engulfed her soul. Her face was distorted with anxiety.

Soko had work to do and could not spend all her time looking after Mother. Therefore, she stayed for only a few days and returned home, thereafter making frequent short visits. When Soko was not around my wife took over her chores, but this proved counterproductive. Mother chose to view Mitsu as the schemer who had got her into this position. Now it was Sadayo she kept following around and pestering about going home.

Mother was more restrained with me. To me she said that it was not that she *had* to rush home, but if it were possible she would *like* to leave that day or the next.

Every night either Soko or my brother made time to visit and keep Mother company; sometimes they both came. At first we had hopes that Mother might get used to Tokyo and resign herself to the change, but gradually we saw that there was no such possibility. Eventually we all came to feel it was cruel to detain her forcibly when she so longed for her own home, and just about then we had a telephone call from my daughter in Karuizawa. She told us that the rainy season had ended that day and the sun had come out. It might be a good time for Granny to visit. I informed her of the state of things in Tokyo and agreed that it would be a fine time for Mother to go to Karuizawa, but I warned her that Mother could be a handful and she must be prepared for that.

"I'll take care of Granny," said my daughter. "I think that nobody else empathizes with her. That's why she gets agitated. I know I can take good care of her. I love Granny and Granny loves me. After all, with an eighty-four-year-old woman one must get into the skin of an eighty-four-year-old to understand her."

I was startled. This was the first time I had ever heard my daughter speak this way. It was as if I, her father, were being chided by my college student daughter for the way I treated my own mother! And yet I detected a certain bravado in her manner, as if she were saying, "All right, I'll take on this Granny that everyone complains about so much, and I'll just show you what I can do." The question remained of how many days such heroism could last.

That night we decided that we would tell Mother about her trip to Karuizawa regardless of the consequences. My graduate student son abruptly went to the heart of the matter. "Granny, go to Karuizawa. It feels good there."

"Karuizawa," Mother responded. "That's nice. If I stayed there a while I would really feel good." When Mother had lived with Soko in Tokyo she had spent some time in Karuizawa; could it be that she had not forgotten?

"Then you *will* go to Karuizawa in two or three days, won't you?" Soko emphasized.

"Of course, I'll go," Mother complied, looking pleased at the prospect.

After much thought, we decided she should go to

Karuizawa by car, and Soko and my younger brother, who understood her best, should accompany her. As Mother got into the car, however, she babbled on about the notion of going home and what was she to do as she hadn't purchased a single gift.

"You're not going home. You're going to Karuizawa," Soko told her.

"Don't joke with me. Karuizawa? Who would want to go there? I'm going home! I'm not going anywhere else." Mother said.

Soko and my brother got on either side of her and half-carried her into the car.

"Don't worry," Soko said to those of us who were seeing them off.

"Well, then," I told the chauffeur, "please take them to their hometown of Karuizawa."

About two days later I left for Karuizawa with Sadayo. It was a little past noon when we reached our destination. We got out of the taxi at the gate of the house, walked up the narrow, gently sloping path flanked by thick groves of trees on either side, and came upon Mother pulling weeds in the garden. Yoshiko was lying on a wicker lounge nearby, my brother was sunbathing on a straw mat in the yard, and Soko was reading a book on the veranda in a position where she could see everyone. Mother's face was cheerful and serene as she looked at Sadayo and me. I felt a sudden relief to see that all was going extremely well in Karuizawa.

"Granny is in a very good mood today. Yesterday she was a little bit naughty but today she's behaving nicely, wouldn't you say?" said Soko, as though she was half-lecturing Mother.

We were told that two days before, when they arrived, possibly owing to fatigue from the long ride, Mother had become half-demented at the realization that she had not been taken to her hometown. She hadn't slept well that night, and Soko and Yoshiko, who slept beside her, couldn't do a thing with her. The next day she had been calm through the morning and had remarked how good it was to be in such a cool place as she walked with her family near the house; yet in the afternoon she had grown troublesome (although not as much as the day before) because, as usual, she demanded to be taken home.

"Today has been the best," Yoshiko said. "It's already past noon but she's so calm in this setting, almost as though she has resigned herself to staying here. And, besides, it's so cool and we sleep so well at night. She slept soundly last night, and I think that's why her mind is rested."

That day Mother did not bring up the subject of going home until evening. Then, in her usual way, she continued to repeat herself, but we no longer attached any importance to the problem. All we had to do was to give her the same answer each time, and although this was depressing it was much easier to deal with than when she got her luggage out and insisted on going home. Listening to Mother's repeated words and our responses merely became a matter of patience and endurance. When she started asking to go home it became a confrontation, a matter of "I want to go home" versus "No, you may not." From Mother's perspective, she couldn't understand why she was denied this wish, while we wondered why she ignored all the explanations we gave her. And the hardest part of all was that each of us found it difficult to stand firm in our denial. Her expression when she demanded to go home was not unlike that of a young child who needs to go home and will accept nothing else. Her desire was expressed in every line of her small body. It was not only her lips, but her eyes, her profile, her back, all revealed the same message.

Mother remained calm for about three days after I arrived and it appeared that Yoshiko had been right in predicting that she would finally grow accustomed to Karuizawa and not think it was such a bad idea after all.

Four days after I arrived, my brother, Soko, and our housekeeper returned to Tokyo and Yoshiko, Sadayo, and I stayed on to look after Mother. Mother saw Soko and the others off at the gate and, as soon as the car was out of sight, said, "It will finally quiet down, won't it? Well, well . . ."

My daughter Yoshiko was shocked. "Oh, Granny, how can you say such a perverse thing!" she said.

"But it's true," Mother laughed. "If you want to go home, you can go, too."

"I *do* want to, but I can't. That's because I have to take care of you, Granny."

"Thanks, but no thanks."

"But it's true. Until you become more reasonable, Sadayo and I must stay with you."

"How can you say such a thing? It's because you know in Tokyo you'll have to get back to your studies."

"My, what impudence!"

Listening to this exchange between grandmother and granddaughter, I thought things would go smoothly now.

However, that evening Mother began packing her things into a bag, the signal that she wanted to go home again. Yoshiko and Sadayo tried to distract her by taking her out for a walk, but to no avail.

From then on Mother's senility reasserted itself. Once she started thinking of going home she seemed unable to control herself. She kept insisting on it and in time came up with plausible reasons. If by some chance the thought left her mind, she became docile and made remarks like, "Pretty soon it will be fall here, won't it?" At those times I was moved by the strange gravity of her profile as she listened to insect sounds pouring forth from the garden.

One day after Mother returned from a walk with my daughter and Sadayo, she suddenly mentioned that they met a woman who asked for directions they could not give, and this woman must be in trouble.

"She did not ask us for directions," Yoshiko said. "She didn't even speak to us, did she? It's just that I said perhaps she may not know her way around here."

"No, she asked me for directions," Mother said seriously.

"That's not true. There was a woman, yes, but she did not ask for directions," Sadayo responded.

"No, I was asked. She must be in great trouble right now, poor thing," Mother insisted.

Judging from her expression, it was clear that Mother believed this to be true. At the dinner table she repeatedly mumbled to herself, "Poor thing. I wonder what she's doing now," and seemed genuinely concerned about that woman.

Some time after dinner Yoshiko came and told me that she could not find Mother. Sadayo and I went out into the garden, but we could not see her. I sent Sadayo to look around the front of the house while I went to the narrow road in back. This road intersected others, leading to the many large villas scattered within the wooded groves in this area. The roads were not private but there was little traffic even during the daytime. Each time I came to an intersection I was confused as to which path to follow. I had absolutely no idea which way Mother had gone.

At one intersection I spotted Mother's diminutive figure running in the distance on one of the roads. The road, hedged in on either side by fir and yew trees, was as straight as if it had been drawn with a ruler. In the distance, where the road narrowed, was Mother. I watched her stop from time to time, then resume running. It may sound strange, but Mother reminded me at that moment of some nimble-footed animal. There was something primeval about her.

When I caught up with her I said nothing other than to tell her to come home. Her expression betrayed her usual embarrassment in such situations, and she said, "I wonder where she went . . . that woman."

These words hit me hard. For the first time it occurred to me that Mother was having hallucinations. Perhaps her yearning to go home had itself become a hallucination.

The incident of the woman seeking directions stayed in Mother's mind only that day; from the next day on, she became quiet and went out into the garden or for walks with Yoshiko and Sadayo. The hallucination may have unsettled her, or perhaps because of the experience her feelings had returned to normal. Now for the first time since she left home, Mother remained calm and quiet for several days.

One day I was on the veranda watching her in the living room with Yoshiko and Sadayo.

"Autumn deepens on the slopes of Mt. Aso,
The desolate view of Mt. Aso at dusk . . . "

Mother chanted in a sing-song voice, then seemed to be trying to recall the rest.

"Granny, you certainly know some unusual things," I said, as I joined them.

"Granny knows a lot of things. Besides 'Kojo Shiragiku,'* she knows 'Ishidomaru.' "** Then Yoshiko prompted

---

*"Kojo Shiragiku," or "Filial Daughter Shiragiku," is a plaintive ballad written by Tetsujiro Inoue in Chinese, translated into Japanese by the poet Naofumi Ochiai, and published in Japan in 1889. Briefly, this medieval tale concerns a young daughter's search for her samurai father after he fails to return from a hunting trip. She flees with her mother to Mt. Aso, where her mother dies, and from there she pursues her search alone. After many trials she is reunited with her father and brother.
**"Ishidomaru," a legendary hero based on a twelfth-century person, was popularized through folk songs, Kabuki, and various traditional

(continued overleaf)

Mother, "Now, Granny, let Father listen to them."
Mother mumbled:

> "Since hearing the message in the wind
>   That Father lives at Mt. Koya,
> Daily have I lain my head
>   Wearily upon the grass pillow . . . "

After these opening lines of the Buddhist hymn to Ishidomaru, she got stuck and said, "I've forgotten it all."

She continued to tilt her head to one side as if racking her brain, then suddenly she looked up and said, "Oh, yes, yes, I also still remember 'A Letter from Jakarta.'"* She then chanted:

> "And still more do I wish to express,
>   Forgetting what at first I should have said,
> Beloved Grandfather and Grandmother,
>   to you have I sent
>   Two bolts of cloth of Holland make . . . "

We all remained silent.

musical forms. Ishidomaru's samurai father, weary of the uncertainties of life, cuts off all family ties and retreats to Mt. Koya. At fourteen, Ishidomaru sets out with his mother from Kyushu for Mt. Koya, where no women are allowed. Ishidomaru sees his father, who, having renounced all worldly ties, denies their relationship. Then the mother dies. The hero returns to Mt. Koya, is taken in as a disciple by his father, and the two enter monastic life together.

*In 1639 the shogunate expelled all Europeans, and their Japanese wives and relatives were banished to Jakarta. Many of these homesick expatriates smuggled messages home, often expressing their yearning for their homeland as well as telling of recent events and of gifts sent.

"And then?" I prompted her.

"I have forgotten everything else. I only remember 'Kojo Shiragiku,' 'Ishidomaru,' and, oh, yes, 'A Letter from Jakarta,'" Mother said gravely.

"Granny, you only recall sad things, don't you?" Yoshiko commented.

Mother merely continued, "I don't remember anything else now." Her expression suggested that nothing more would come forth no matter how hard she tried.

"It's 'the pain of parting from loved ones,'* isn't it?" I said, immediately taken aback by the words I had uttered. To me it seemed that Mother's soul was obsessed with the pain of parting from loved ones. She herself had entered into her own drama on this theme. Was not her yearning to return home similar to the suffering of the homesick author of "A Letter from Jakarta?" And was it not possible that her concern for the young woman she imagined to be lost and troubled was the same as the sadness engraved in her heart when she first came to know the dramas of Ishidomaru and Kojo Shiragiku as a young woman?

I have written how my brother-in-law Akio once remarked that Mother's interests had gradually been reduced to marriage, birth, and death. Well, stated in these terms it could also be said that her attention now was fixated on "the pain of parting from loved ones." In a person's life marriage, birth, and death do play a large part, but over

*One of the eight worldly sufferings, according to Buddhist philosophy.

life's entire span what remains indelible of human relationships until the very end is "the pain of parting from loved ones." Had Mother, after living for over eight decades, reached a point where her mind and body registered only these things? At times hatred showed on her aged face, but it lasted only a moment and was erased immediately. I felt that what remained alive in her withered-leaf of a body and her damaged mind was distilled, like water from which all impurities have been removed—feelings characterized by some transparency and the utmost simplicity.

That night I had some whiskey with guests on the veranda. They left at about nine o'clock, then three others arrived. I joined the new visitors and had some more to drink, and it was after two in the morning when they left.

When I returned to the veranda after seeing my guests off at the gate I found Mother, who had come out in her night clothes, and Yoshiko, also in her nightgown, arguing about Granny's going back to sleep. Apparently Mother could not sleep and wished to come out to the veranda in her night clothes, but I would not permit this because the night air was chilly. I moved to a seat in the living room and sat across from Mother for a while. I had some more whiskey.

"Well, Granny, you can repeat yourself all you want. I'm drunk tonight, so it won't bother me in the least," I said.

I truly felt that way then. It had been some years since I had sat face to face with Mother with an open mind. I usually did my best to blot out her repetitive remarks, forcing myself to swallow the admonishments that were on the tip of my tongue. Usually, to sit across from Mother meant an ongoing struggle within myself. But that night, thanks to my drunken state, I felt I could sit there with an open mind, and I said this.

As it was, the next morning Yoshiko said, "Last night, Father, you were drunk, weren't you? Granny told me so. She said, 'That man is strange, he keeps repeating himself.'"

I laughed. I had no recollection of what I had said and I naturally did not remember what Mother had said either.

"It's very doubtful, Father, whether Granny thinks you are her child," Yoshiko went on. "She keeps referring to you as 'that man' in a most contemptuous way."

During Mother's stay in Karuizawa Shikako called every five or six days from her home. Although Shikako had entrusted Mother to our care, she apparently still felt concern for her.

After several phone calls Shikako said, "I think Akio will be discharged from the hospital by the end of August and it would be a great help if you would keep Granny until mid-September. As it probably gets cold earlier up in Karuizawa, I'll send her some more kimono." Then, remarking that she could hear Granny's voice in the background, she ended the conversation.

As it was, however, Mother returned home around mid-August. Sadayo, the young woman who had so long cared for Mother, was recalled to the village on sudden business, and this greatly influenced Mother's return. She was incredibly intuitive in such matters, and from the time she began to sense that Sadayo was going to leave Karuizawa, the heartrending homesickness of the author of "A Letter from Jakarta" again assailed Mother. No one knew how she sensed that Sadayo was leaving, but she began packing her bags and at times tried to set off for the bus station with only the clothes on her back. No one could do anything with her any longer. Finally she started complaining that she would rather die than stay on in such a place.

Such a statement from her grandmother came as quite a blow to Yoshiko. "I'm cutting off all ties with you, Granny," Yoshiko said seriously.

"I'll say bye-bye to you, too," Mother retorted hotly. We were astonished that Mother even knew this foreign expression.

It was mid-August when Soko and my brother came to fetch Mother. As it was, she had spent almost a month at Karuizawa. On the day Mother left, Yoshiko, standing in front of the lavatory mirror, remarked, "In her last telephone call Aunt Shikako said she's gained some weight. Well, thanks to her, I think I've lost some."

After Mother returned to the country she settled down and became quiet. It was as if, having arrived at the place of her incessant demands, she had no further requirements or desires to focus on.

After I left Karuizawa in the fall I went to Izu to see Mother. I had wanted to make some sarcastic comments to the effect that she should have no more complaints now that she was home, but her condition was totally different from what I expected. She had quite forgotten that she had been in Tokyo or in Karuizawa.

"Karuizawa!" she exclaimed. "I certainly would like to be taken to such a lovely place." Asked whether she could remember ever being there, she replied that it was not a question of her remembering since she had never been there.

"Well, what about the time before? Remember, you did go there before, didn't you?"

"No, I've never been there. I had thought for some time that I really would like to go, but at my age . . . "

So she had also forgotten about the time she had gone some years before. She had remembered it when she was last in Tokyo, but in this short space of time that recollection also vanished. Her physical vigor, on the other hand, had completely returned, and what with that and her cheerful demeanor she looked like a different person from the one we saw in Karuizawa. By contrast, Keiichi, or America-san, had completely deteriorated during Mother's absence. Walking now tired him so that it was a real chore for him to visit Mother. In the time it took him to get to Mother's house—always accompanied by my aunt— Mother was capable of making several round trips.

"How I envy Granny her sturdy legs!" Keiichi said, whenever he did come.

With the weakening of his legs, Uncle's visits decreased and Mother took to barging into America-san's home two and even three times a day. At times she returned home in a bad mood, vowing she would never go there again (perhaps she had been reprimanded about something), but in an hour she would forget her pique and set off again.

In her own home Mother seemed to do precisely as she pleased, with an air that might, without exaggeration, be called downright arrogant.

"She's turned into a thoroughly spoiled little girl, and it's no use saying anything to her because she won't listen," Shikako complained.

At the end of autumn a Buddhist memorial service was held on the fiftieth anniversary of the death of Granny Onui, the woman who had raised me and been my surrogate mother when I left my parents' home at an early age. Although I called her Granny we were not related. Onui had been a mistress of my great-grandfather, and after his death she had been formally entered into our family register as a branch family; thus, on paper, Mother was her adopted daughter. Because of these complicated relationships and because my young mother had viewed Granny Onui as a disturbance to the family peace as well as an interloper, the two women never got along well and Mother could not possibly have had any affection for her.

Yet on Granny Onui's fiftieth anniversary service, Mother had totally forgotten both the foster mother and her own ill feelings. "Oh, yes, it's Onui's memorial service, isn't it?" She mouthed these words but gave no hint that this woman called Onui had in fact been her long-time adversary.

I reacted to the situation with considerable emotion. I was a sixth grader in elementary school when this grandmother died. I clearly remembered the day of the funeral, and the fifty years which I myself had lived since then seemed long. But what made that time span seem longer still was seeing how completely all feelings of either obligation or vengeance had vanished from Mother's mind.

To Mother as she was now, it did not matter whose memorial service was being held. She seemed pleased at the mere fact that people had gathered together, and she was liberal with her charm as she greeted each guest. "It was so good of you to come, especially when you're so busy."

"Granny, it's wonderful that you're in such good health." All the visitors said the same thing. Some of them really believed this, but others added, " . . . well, at least, in such good physical health."

Uncle Keiichi shared his reminiscences about Granny Onui during the banquet following the memorial service. Whether he had liked or disliked her was unclear, but by then he was the only person remaining who had known her well, although he had left Japan at a young age. Mother also attended the banquet. I sat at a distance and observed her. She seemed to be listening to Keiichi from time to time, but she was frequently distracted, and whenever she spoke to Sadayo, who was there to look after her, she was reprimanded. Each time she was scolded she would glance meekly at Keiichi, and as she did so her face looked even younger and more ingenuous than that of the twenty-three-year-old Sadayo.

One day in mid-January, after not having met for some time, my brother and sisters and I gathered together at the country home to celebrate Mother's eighty-fifth birthday. On this occasion Shikako prefaced her report to us with the statement that she had had a shock. "You know that Granny has been calling me 'Grandmother' since some time last year. I thought at first that she was calling me Grandmother because my grandchildren from Mishima call me that, but I don't think that's it at all. She really seems to think that I am Grandmother."

"I wonder who in the world she is mistaking you for," my brother said.

"I don't think it's anyone in particular, just a grand-mother in general."

"Yes, that *would* be a shock."

"When your own mother starts seeing you as an old woman, you're over the hill, wouldn't you say?"

"I wonder if she knows you're her daughter."

"Sometimes she does seem to think of me as her daughter, but the reverse seems to occur more frequently. If she's like that with me, in America-san's case she must truly believe that he and her brother Keiichi are two dif-ferent people. Uncle himself has completely accepted this recently, and now he begins his discussions with her with, 'You probably won't understand anything I say, but there is a person called Keiichi who is your brother and this is about him. . . . ' It's amusing to hear that," Shikako had said.

Since around the end of the year Mother had had fre-quent hallucinations. Even when there were no visitors she prepared tea for guests. At times she had the notion that guests were present and the tea she made was for them; at other times it appeared she confused the current day with the previous day and was preparing tea for yesterday's visitors.

As we discussed Mother, concentrating on Shikako's report, Mother herself sat in a daze in the adjoining living room.

"Granny, we're all talking about you!" Soko called out to her.

"Of course, I know that," Mother laughed innocently. "You're gossiping about me, aren't you? What else would you do?"

Her expression, as she responded, was pleasant. Then she immediately lapsed back into her stupor and submerged herself in her own thoughts. I wondered what she could be thinking. Her past and present were blurred, and reality was confused with hallucination. Now and then she would emerge from her world to take in something of what her children were saying, but those words also faded away in a moment.

"Gossamer spring fly,
   Our only difference lies
In my living
   Outside the mound."*

*The spring fly, an insect resembling a dragonfly, lives only a day after it emerges from its mound. There is indeed a gossamer quality to the sight of swarms of spring flies winging out of their mounds on a sunny day. The author here is trying to convey his mother's glimmering awareness of past and present, the living and the dead.

I quoted Joso's* poem which appears in Akutagawa's** essay "Obituaries" (1926).

"Fantasies must chase about the withered fields,"*** my brother responded, as though completing the poem.

In early May, Uncle Keiichi died suddenly. There had been nothing particularly wrong with him beyond the physical deterioration that had become a great deal more noticeable that year and could be attributed to the wear and tear of aging. The apparent cause of his death was the strain of forcing himself to accompany his wife on a shopping trip to Numazu. On their way home he felt nauseated and dizzy, and as soon as they returned to the house he went to bed, but in the night Uncle drew his last breath. He died all too quickly—not yet two years since his return to Japan. Unlike Mother he had shown no signs of senility. Could it be that after all the hassles he had with her, he elected to remove himself from this life before he became like her?

It was sprinkling rain on the morning of his funeral, but the skies cleared around the time we left for the crematorium. To get there, the funeral procession had to climb a rather steep hill called Mt. Kumano. The road, with its exposed stones, was damp and slippery, and walk-

*A Japanese poet (1662–1704) and disciple of the famous poet Basho.
**Ryunosuke Akutagawa (1892–1927) was a writer of short stories, one of which is the famous *Rashomon*. He is well known for his brilliant prose and for his intellectual, nihilistic philosophy.
***This line is borrowed from one of Basho's (1644–94) *haiku*.

ing was difficult; but the trees lining both sides of the road glowed a vivid green after the rain. At Father's funeral and again at Granny Onui's funeral I had climbed this hilly road in the same way. And at the funerals of several of Mother's brothers and sisters, I had also joined the procession and climbed up this hill. Now only my mother, the eldest, and Maki, the youngest, remained; everyone in between was gone.

After Uncle's funeral urn was buried and his wooden plaque set in place, the Buddhist sutra read, and the incense burnt, Soko and I left the group and went to our family plot a short distance away to visit Father's grave. There were five gravestones there in the rectangular plot bounded by a hedge of dwarf cedars: Father's, Granny Onui's, Shunma's, Takenori's, and a small blank one. I had previously been told that the nameless stone marked the grave of an infant who died shortly after birth, the child of an assistant physician who worked for my great-grandfather. Shunma and Takenori's headstones were appropriately small, in keeping with their status as young men who died early. I peered to make out their death dates. They were hard to see, for the characters were worn down and covered with moss. At length I determined that Shunma's death date was September 1894 and Takenori's was 1898. Since Mother was born in 1885, Shunma died when she was ten, according to the old Japanese method of calculating, and Takenori when she was fourteen. When I informed Soko of this, she laughed and said, "Granny certainly was precocious, wasn't she?"

"Then there was no need for Grandpa to be jealous," I said. "But Grandpa probably never would have guessed that after his death his own wife would flaunt her early attachments so shamelessly."

As I washed the surface of the tombstone of my unsuspecting father and Soko pulled out weeds surrounding it, a thought struck me. "He *didn't* know, did he?" I remarked.

That night there was a funeral party for relatives and neighbors. Because America-san's Western home was small, the reception room of the head family's house across from his was chosen for the purpose.

Mother arrived during the banquet. When I heard her voice coming from the kitchen where the neighbors' wives were working, I got up and went to her.

"Is it true that it was Keiichi who died? Why didn't you let me know?" Mother demanded vehemently of the women. She was pale and her gaze was steady, as was usually the case when she was excited.

"Granny, you knew about it, didn't you?" someone said.

"No, I certainly did not. I just heard," Mother replied.

Her heavy breathing as she spoke suggested that she had really just learned of Keiichi's death and had run right over. Shikako came in then. She began urging Mother to go home, and Mother began to press her.

"Why did you hide Keiichi's death from me?" she asked. She was serious.

"I didn't hide it from you at all. Didn't you yourself say that it was sad about America-san?" Shikako replied.

Mother shook her head vigorously and said, "No, I didn't know."

Shikako and I escorted Mother home. Five minutes later there was a commotion and someone said that Mother was gone, that we had to go out to search for her. I went to the banquet, but she was not there. Then, on a hunch, I went to America-san's house. My aunt apparently had elected to avoid the confusion of the banquet by staying home, and I was rewarded by a glimpse of Mother's diminutive figure seated in the living room facing my aunt. As Shikako and I entered the room, my aunt said, "Granny just offered incense."

At the end of the room, by the Buddhist altar, was a black-ribboned picture of Keiichi surrounded with flowers. As my aunt came forward to meet us, she said, "Granny is crying for him." As we approached Mother, we observed that her face was wet with tears.

We took her home again, but during the night she visited America-san's home two more times and sat in front of the altar there. Once Sadayo accompanied her, and the other time a neighbor's wife helping at the party brought her. Both had been badgered by Mother until they could not refuse.

"Granny is genuinely grieving, isn't she?" Sadayo re-marked. "Her expression is different from usual. She seems to think that both America-san and Keiichi have died. I wonder . . . does she think the daytime funeral service was for America-san and the banquet in the evening for Keiichi?" she mused aloud.

I could not believe this theory, but it was hard to account for Mother's detachment at the daytime service and her heartfelt grief in the evening in any other way. Sadayo had looked after Mother for many years and had made her own evaluation. Whether her point of view was accurate or not I could not say, but one thing that night was clear: despite the confusion in her mind, Mother's grief over one person's death had touched her heart. During the ceremonial occasion—if one could call the confusion at the funeral banquet a ceremonial occasion—Mother was perhaps the saddest of all the mourners.

By the time I came downstairs the following morning Mother had already gone to America-san's home. When I went after her I found both the old women—my aunt and my mother—in front of the new Buddhist tablet with swollen eyes. They looked like a pair of deeply attached sisters.

Because my aunt was already fatigued, I tried my best to keep Mother from going over, but Mother would not listen. When no one was watching, she slipped out. Normally my aunt did not particularly welcome Mother's visits, but her grief at the loss of her husband was such that she did not turn Mother away no matter how frequent her visits became. She seemed to have a need even for Mother. Whenever Mother could not be seen, Shikako usually said, "Oh dear, Granny's gone to America-san's again." Once she reported, "Granny's impossible to deal with because she can run faster than I can. In fact, a little while ago she stopped and waited for me to catch up."

I stayed for two days after the funeral, then returned to Tokyo to attend a meeting, leaving my wife, Mitsu, behind. I went directly to the meeting from Tokyo Station and by the time I reached home it was close to midnight. No sooner had I arrived than I heard the telephone ring. The call was from Mitsu, with the message that a friend was scheduled to call on her in Tokyo the next day and would I please cancel that visit. Then she added, "Granny created a great rumpus a short while ago."

"Did she collapse?" I asked quickly.

"No, not that, but she . . . she went to bed, then got up in a very agitated state saying she had put you to bed beside her and you had disappeared. She went out, and we brought her back very shortly."

"By 'you' do you mean me?"

"Yes, that's right. It seems you have become an infant again."

"That can't be true."

"Well, it is true, though, because she did say that she had put Yasushi to bed but he had disappeared and she became very agitated. . . . In any case, I was startled. It was late at night when she disappeared. She went looking for you."

"Where was she?"

"They said she was walking toward Nagano from the corner hardware store."

"Who brought her back?"

"Shikako and Sadayo."

I felt a sudden chill. In my mind I saw the road leading to Nagano reflected in the piercing white light of the moon.

On one side were paddy fields a level higher than the road, and on the other side were more paddy fields, but that side was terraced and the terraces ended in a ravine. Bathed in the white light of the moon, Mother was walking along this road. She was looking for me, the infant.

"I'll hang up now," I told my wife.

After I put down the receiver I stood there a while, feeling unsettled. An overwhelming urge to go somewhere came over me. In a sense, if Mother was out looking for me, then I, too, must find Mother. I was born in Asahikawa in Hokkaido, lived there for only three months, then was taken by Mother to her family home. If her actions now were based on hallucinations about that period, then I was one, and if I was a year old Mother was twenty-three.

In my mind's eye I conjured up a picture of myself as an infant with my twenty-three-year-old mother walking along a road bathed in moonlight, searching for me. And there was another image—of myself past my sixtieth year, searching for my eighty-five-year-old mother on the same road. One picture was permeated by a chilling quality, the other by a certain awesomeness. These two images, however, immediately became juxtaposed and merged. There was I as an infant and there was my twenty-three-year-old mother; there was my sixty-three-year-old self and there was my eighty-five-year-old mother with her aged face. The years 1907 and 1969 came together and the sixty years converged, then diffused in the light of the moon. The chill and the awe also fused and were penetrated by the piercing light of the moon.

After I calmed down I became aware that as I talked to Mitsu on the telephone a picture had formed in my mind. The road to Nagano, which appeared in my mind's eye, was one I knew well as a young boy. It was the road I traveled daily to go swimming in the river. There was now an elementary school beside the road as well as a dairy. Very recently, as I recall, a stationery store also appeared on that road.

Be that as it may, I thought that Mother had returned to her twenty-third year and was now living in that world. If Mother was twenty-three, then Uncle would be nineteen, and it would be two years before he set sail for America. The Mother who mourned Uncle's death so deeply was the twenty-three-year-old girl mourning her nineteen-year-old brother.

I went to the telephone and called. Shikako answered. When I asked after Mother, she informed me that she had been given a pill and was sleeping soundly.

"After alarming everyone, the party in question is sleeping like a young girl," she said. "Perhaps it was the medication that made her snore loudly until just a while ago, but right now she's not snoring and is sleeping peacefully. She'll probably get up early in the morning and go to America-san's home again."

The Surface
of
the Snow

On the evening of November 21 the selection committee of a certain literary award met at a restaurant in Shimbashi, central Tokyo. After deciding the award should go to O, a leading writer, we had a relaxed banquet. However, I left halfway through the party. I felt somewhat under the weather and I also wanted to be quietly by myself in my own study at home.

I had some tea in the living room, then went straight to my study. My bedding had been laid out for me there, but I sat wide awake in front of my desk. The deadlines for installments of two serialized works in a couple of magazines were approaching, but my schedule called for starting them the next day and I wished to keep to that. Instead I decided to use the short time available to me that night to write a review of the work which had been chosen for the literary award.

I had to write it within a few days anyway and I thought I might as well get it out of the way. Of the page and a half allotted me I filled one page writing about the author's work. Although there was still space, I did not touch on the works of other candidates but stopped.

Just then a call came from my sister Shikako, who was living with Mother in our family home in Izu. My wife, Mitsu, took the call, then immediately transferred it to the study. Shikako reported that Mother's condition had suddenly taken a turn for the worse, a doctor had been called in, and Mother was now being fed intravenously.

"I really don't anticipate any sudden change, but her frailty . . . " Shikako's voice trailed off. She said she would call again in about an hour to give me the latest news and hung up. It was a little past nine.

Mother had by now advanced to the grand age of eighty-nine, and since she was born in February she would mark off another year in less than three months. Although there was nothing specifically wrong with her, the process of aging had put her in and out of bed throughout the past year. Her health was basically good, and it seemed as though she could still last another five to ten years; yet when she caught a cold there was a frailty about her which suggested she could easily slip through death's door.

In preparation for an emergency, I told Mitsu to retire early and decided I would take the call from home. Around ten-thirty I received the second call from Shikako. "Mother is sleeping, but her breathing is labored and I'm having the doctor stay with her. Because it's Mother, I think that if she makes it through the night she'll probably be all right tomorrow, but I'm a bit apprehensive about tonight." Shikako was composed. Her voice, however, was lower and softer than usual.

I doubted Mother's condition would worsen that suddenly, but before I hung up I told Shikako that whatever the case I would leave Tokyo the following morning as soon as I could arrange for a car.

I thereupon immediately set to work preparing for my trip. Since I figured I would probably have to spend a few days there, I packed the necessary books for the two serial pieces I had to write. And because on the twenty-fifth there was to be a ceremony for the opening of a library for my works built in the outskirts of Numazu by hometown friends, I also packed my formal, black, double-breasted suit and some shirts.

At one-fifty in the morning, Shikako called for the third time. "Granny just stopped breathing . . . ten minutes ago," she said. Then I heard my sister sob. After her weeping subsided, I thanked her formally for looking after Mother for so long and said that Mother was surely very happy to have been cared for to the very end by Shikako and her husband, that Shikako of all her children had done the most for her. These words were meant as an expression of appreciation from a brother to his sister, as well as of condolence. Then I told her we would settle everything the following morning after I arrived, and with this our conversation ended.

I went to Mitsu's bedroom to notify her of Mother's death. She wasn't asleep, for she arose immediately. The telephone was ringing when I returned to the study. It was my youngest sister Soko, who lived in Tokyo. Her voice was surprisingly strong. We arranged that she should come to my house at eight in the morning and we would go together by car.

As I watched Mitsu place Mother's photograph on the family Buddhist altar and prepare for the burning of incense in the living room, I thought, "Well, Mother has finally died," and felt shaken by it. I am not sure how much time elapsed before I heard the telephone ring again in my study. I had the call transferred to the living room, picked up the phone, and once again it was Shikako. She said the wake would take place the next day—although there were only a few hours left before daybreak—and although the funeral would ordinarily be held the day after that, as it was inauspicious the funeral would be conducted the following day, the twenty-fourth. She wanted me to know this as well as to find out if it would be convenient. Relatives had already gathered around Mother's deathbed and begun to make plans. Perhaps because she was keyed up, Shikako's voice sounded strong, different from her earlier call. I told her that even if she could not sleep she should go to bed and try to get some rest.

After that call I discussed the following day's arrangements with Mitsu. Soko and I would leave first and Mitsu would notify all our married children, make preparations to leave the house vacant for a few days, and then leave Tokyo in time for the wake. And since the amount of luggage might be considerable, it would be best to load it all in my car.

I packed my funeral clothes into a bag and decided to leave the rest to Mitsu and make myself a drink. Although very little time had elapsed since Mother's death, its aftermath—the funeral—was already taking shape, and my planned trip to see her had been transformed into a funeral mission.

I sat in front of my desk and drank my whiskey in the study. It seemed only fit and proper that on the night a man hears of his mother's death there should be a dialogue between mother and son, but I could not get into the mood. Mother had lived a long life and had finally died.

She was now sleeping peacefully—lying quietly with her eyes closed, never to wake up again. Those were my only thoughts. When Father had died fifteen years before, at the age of eighty, and I had been told the news in the same study, I had sat in front of the same desk waiting for the night to end. I had thought of several things that I, as a son, had wanted to say to Father, things I should have told him before his death but never had. In Mother's case, however, it was different. I had said everything I wanted to say to her while she was still alive, and there was nothing left.

Soko arrived at eight-thirty. Hearing her voice, I went into the living room and found her talking to Mitsu. As I entered, Soko said, "Granny died suddenly, didn't she? If I had known it would be so sudden, I would have gone to see her last Sunday." Soko was expressing her sorrow in these words.

Just as I had thanked Shikako the previous night for caring for Mother so many years, I also thanked Soko. "You have done a lot for Granny, and Granny . . . well, I don't know whether I should say this or not . . . "

"She didn't suffer a long illness," Soko said. "She died very quickly, and I think the way she died was very much in character for her: 'I am now carefree and at ease and you folks may not know this, but I am in a comfortable place . . . '" She ended by speaking for Mother. Soko covered her eyes.

After a hasty breakfast, Soko and I brought our many bags to the entrance. For me, there was a bag with clothes for the opening ceremony of the library as well as one with funeral clothes. Owing to the circumstances I could not but take time off from my work, but there was nothing I could do about the opening ceremony of the library because invitations had already been sent by the sponsors. The funeral was to be on the twenty-fourth, a day before the library ceremony, and although it would be very difficult for me to control my feelings that day, at least I could be grateful that the two events did not overlap.

It was close to ten when we finally left the house. As the car moved onto the Tokyo–Nagoya Highway, the sky was beautifully clear and Mt. Fuji was exquisite.

"Granny would have had her birthday in just a short time," Soko remarked. In the New Year Mother would have turned ninety, according to the old Japanese way of counting. My family had discussed a birthday party for her and, incidentally, had made general plans to stop by our country house to spend a few days with her after attending the library ceremony on the twenty-fifth, but all those plans were foiled by her sudden death. As far as Mother was concerned, however, a part of her might well have said, "If you're coming to see me simply as an afterthought to some library ceremony, I'm not greatly pleased."

When I brought up this notion to Soko, she said, "Well, yes, given Granny's personality, I wouldn't be surprised if she had actually refused to see us if she thought our visit was incidental to the ceremony. But as far as the funeral is concerned, everyone will be gathering just for her, so she should have no complaints. I'm sure she'd like a lively funeral. She'd be delighted if a lot of people attended."

From the vicinity of Gotemba we saw Mt. Fuji first on our right, then in front of us, then to our left. The mountain was bare from peak to foothills. It was the first time I had ever seen it so.

As we approached Numazu, Mt. Fuji was again to our right, then we left it behind. The sky was a limpid blue, with floating white clouds like balls of raw cotton. From May through June of that year I had traveled in Iran and Turkey, and I now recalled how the beauty of the clear blue skies and pure white clouds in southern Turkey seemed to pierce my very soul. That day on the Tokyo–Nagoya Highway the sky and clouds were just like those in Turkey. It occurred to me how very much in character it was for Mother to choose to die on such a day.

I have previously written about Mother's process of aging in two parts, entitled "Under the Blossoms" and "The Light of the Moon." In the former Mother had reached the age of eighty and in the latter she was eighty-five. She had lived more than four years beyond the time described in "The Light of the Moon." In the final period her senility had worsened during the first two years and she continued to create problems for the family. But in her last two years of life her senility seemed to lose its force, in conjunction with her physical decline. Although her mental deterioration did not stop, her days became incredibly calm. In this respect she gained some respite, and so did her children.

In "The Light of the Moon," I described how Mother gradually erased from her memory the life she had lived during her seventies, then her sixties, then her fifties, and so on, until she eventually returned, in her mind, to somewhere between her teens and early twenties. A year after I completed the work Mother came to Tokyo to stay with me for about twenty days while my sister Shikako was away on urgent business. It was the cold season, and my wife, Mitsu, and my younger daughter, Yoshiko, a recent college graduate, went to the country to fetch Mother. They stayed overnight at the Izu house, returning to Tokyo by car the following day.

Mother was in a good mood when she left the country. She went around saying her goodbyes to the neighbors and telling them she would be away for a while, then bustled into the car and appeared to enjoy the wintry view en route. But within an hour of settling down in Tokyo she began demanding to be taken back, and for the duration of her visit she never let up on the subject.

In the morning, perhaps because she was rested, her manner of speaking was gentle and she made plausible remarks such as, "It's about time for me to think of leaving today," or "I have a fine, carefree life here as a guest, but I'm concerned about what's going on at home . . . " From noon to evening, however, the urge to go home consumed her and someone had to watch her at all times. Whenever she was left alone for a few minutes, she packed her little bag and made for the front door. She would not listen to any explanations, and if anyone so much as touched her shoulder she flew into a rage and acted as if she had been assaulted. Of all those in the family she was most compliant toward me, but in her extremely agitated state in the afternoon she would not listen even to me; indeed at such times I seriously doubted whether she realized I was her own son.

Toward the end of each day though, when dusk began to fall, she calmed down. Why this happened was not clear. Perhaps she thought it was then too late to go home, or perhaps she was simply exhausted from her afternoon's agitation. For whatever reason, her face became serene, and she went out into the chilly air of the garden, peered into my library, and, surprisingly, allowed herself to be bathed submissively. After that she usually dined with the family.

"Granny, you created quite a rumpus today," the children often said, to which she usually replied, "What nonsense! It was you who made the commotion!"

She did not, however, forget her desire to go home. She made various remarks to the effect that she would be leaving the next morning on the early train so we didn't have to see her off, she would say goodbye that night; or tomorrow many people would be waiting anxiously for her return.

"Who are all those people who will be waiting for you?" Mitsu once asked, to which Mother responded sarcastically, "It's quite different from this house. We have a lot of help, the garden is very large, and since our bathwater is drawn from the hot springs, I can bathe without troubling others."

"Goodness, Granny's house is splendid, isn't it!" Yoshiko remarked.

She softened her tone for Yoshiko. "Come and visit me sometime. We have a lot of fruit trees. Our kitchen is much larger than the one here, and we even have two wells." When Mother spoke like this, she reminded me of a young girl boasting about her own home.

After dinner Mother usually sat for about two hours on a cushion on the living room carpet, at times listening to the family conversation and at other times drifting off into her own world. Soon she became drowsy and nodded off, and whenever she came to, she put her hands to her kimono collar and looked slightly embarrassed.

As soon as Yoshiko became aware that Mother was sleepy she got up quickly and took her hand, saying, "Well, it's night-night time." If Mother refused to go, Yoshiko said, "Naughty-naughty, now, it's night-night time," and proceeded to get Mother on her feet and half-carry her up the stairs leading to the bedrooms. It was Yoshiko's task to put Mother to bed, and it was her special talent. If anyone else attempted it there was great resistance, for in this matter Mother was indulgent only toward Yoshiko—although during the day when Mother was agitated she was more unkind to Yoshiko than to any of us. I had never seen Yoshiko put Mother to bed, but at times Yoshiko talked about it, saying that things went smoothly one night or not so well another night.

"I do it very quickly. I help her take off her kimono, put on her night kimono, get her under the covers, tuck her in, then pat her on the shoulders. Then I get some tissues, her wallet, and a flashlight, show them to her and tell her I have placed these items by her, and set them down by her pillow. Then I pat her on the shoulders again. She does not seem to settle down unless I do this. Then I go out into the hall, switch off her light so that only her room is dark, and stand there a while. If she doesn't get up within two or three minutes, then she's fine." Yoshiko probably put Mother to bed in that manner every night. I liked listening to Yoshiko talk about it. Her conversation captured the intimacy between that singular pair—grandmother and granddaughter.

Once Yoshiko said, "Do you know who Granny thinks I am? Her servant. It certainly seems like that. And I have the impression that she also thinks of me as an *older* serving woman. She wheedles and she gets angry and, last night for instance, after giving me no end of trouble, she said, 'Thank you very much. Why don't you ask permission to retire, too?' "

I have written of how we came to the conclusion that Mother was gradually rubbing off—as though with an eraser—the long line of her eighty-plus years of life and had finally reached a stage somewhere between her teens and early twenties. We saw no reason to change that view now, except that in observing her daytime behavior it was difficult to deal with her simply as if she were a girl again. When she was clamoring about going home, her words and actions betrayed a skill at bargaining and manipulation typical of a worldly-wise woman. Thus, although Mother seemed to be living within her experiences of girlhood in her comparatively tractable moments, one part of her that had lived for a long time emerged, making it impossible for her to remain docile.

The most notable change from her behavior of two or three years earlier was that she no longer talked about Shunma and Takenori, the young, romantic idols of her teens who had been the cause of much teasing by her grandchildren. If the children broached the subject, that was another matter; but she herself did not bring it up. Apparently her aging had progressed to the stage when even those boyish faces had dimmed in her memory.

As I listened to Yoshiko saying she thought Granny was mistaking her for a serving woman, I wondered whether Mother, in her docile moments, had regressed to her early years when she was thoroughly spoiled by an indulgent grandfather. She was not yet in her teens when she became enamored of the two boys, Shunma and Takenori; if she no longer talked about them, it probably meant she had regressed to an even earlier age.

When Mother was about five or six she was taken into her grandfather's home. He had two private practices, one in Mishima and the other in our Izu hometown. Her grandparents were childless and had adopted a married couple to carry on the family name. When Mother came along, the first-born daughter of this couple, he became deeply attached to her and took her away from her parents to raise her in the Izu town where he had one of his practices. It seems that as early as then he intended her to start a branch family: marry a man who would take the family name and carry on the family medical tradition. Indeed, his plans became reality after some years. In any case, because of her grandfather's blind affection for her, Mother was raised in an atmosphere that might be called abnormal, and it appears that all her acquired personality was formed during this period. She was never happy unless she was the center of attention; she had a strong pride; and there was a part of her that seemed to expect others to wait on her. But I suspect her natural disposition was rather different; she could also be fiercely compassionate, highly organized, and conciliatory. These contrasting tendencies came to the fore at different times in her long life. Some saw Mother as a gentle person while others found her cruel. Some thought of her as self-centered and willful; others saw her pleasant and sociable side. The only trait which everyone agreed on was her inordinate pride.

At the thought that Mother might have regressed to those early years when she lacked for nothing and was completely pampered by her grandfather, I felt a sense of lightness, perhaps a sort of relief. To be sure, at the age of five or six, or perhaps seven or eight, she would likely be more childlike, even incorrigibly willful. But speaking as a son, I would rather that her senility carry her to her childhood than any other period because childhood had probably been the happiest time in her life. If she could live with the sense of life as it was then, she should experience no oppression and gloom. During the day she was now so glum she depressed everyone around her. I hoped for her

because she couldn't find the bathroom, but that wasn't it at all. From my room she goes to the toilet, then returns to her own room and goes to sleep. It's on her way to the bathroom that she visits my room."

"She's concerned and checking to see whether you're in or not," Yoshiko said.

"It's no joke. I have to work and I have to get up early. Does she go to your room?" he asked Yoshiko.

"She came once. But she hasn't come since."

"Maybe it's not that she doesn't come, but you're asleep and don't know about it," my younger son said.

Then my children expressed various opinions as to whether Mother was foggy with sleep, suffered from somnambulism, or was acting out some of her hallucinations.

"Well, whatever it is, it's not pleasant to be awakened in the middle of the night," said my elder son. "Once, not long ago, she dropped her flashlight. I got up and helped her search for it, but we just couldn't find it until, on a hunch, I checked under my bed and there it was. Even the flashlight has begun to float away by itself, right?"

"That can't be," Mother suddenly interjected.

We all looked at her.

"How can a flashlight start moving by itself?" She was seated on her bedding, wrapped in the quilted robe that Yoshiko had forced on her. She had completely forgotten about going downstairs, and for a while had looked extremely mortified as well as displeased at finding herself the center of our discussion. As far as we could tell she had listened only to a part of it—to what my elder son had just said—and finding it amusing, had suddenly joined in the conversation. Her previous petulant but confused expression had given way to the cheerful and innocent smile of a very young girl. It was enough to rob the rest of us of all ill feeling. Mother was soon put to bed by Yoshiko, and my sons and I went to our own rooms, as if Mother had given us the order to disperse.

A few days later Mother again tried to make her way to my room late at night. I was again at my desk, and I heard her stealthy steps cross the carpet in the adjacent room. I stood up immediately and looked into the living room. The door leading to the front entrance was half-open and, perhaps owing to the lighting on the stairs, the furniture in that area alone was dimly outlined while the rest of the room was pitch dark. In the middle of that darkness stood Mother with her flashlight and, behind her, Yoshiko in a blue gown, swaying with sleepiness.

"Ghosts!" I blurted, for the two figures standing in the middle of the large Western-style room did indeed resemble spirits. The previous year, when I had gone to China, I had seen a play called *Love and Harmony* at the Shanghai Theater. There was a scene in it in which Lung-wang, his midget attendant, and the spirit of the heroine ride on a cloud and fly toward the capital along the Yangtze River. Mother, as she searched the study entrance with her flashlight, resembled the midget shining his long torch into the netherworld, while Yoshiko, because of the cast of her blue gown, reminded me of the woman who had been turned into a spirit.

"It's hard on you, isn't it?" I said to Yoshiko.

"I'm so sleepy, and she woke me up! I thought she'd return to her own room, but she started coming downstairs. I couldn't leave her alone, could I? It's so dangerous. She looked into Mother's room before she came here," she added.

"I wonder if she's searching for someone."

"I don't think so. I think she's lonesome. When she wakes up at night she might think she's not in her own room. And I think she goes from room to room telling herself that it's not the right one," Yoshiko remarked.

I did not feel drowsy after I walked Mother and Yoshiko upstairs, so I brought a bottle of whiskey into the study and pondered on what might be going on in my Mother's senile head to make her behave thus late at night. Perhaps, as Yoshiko surmised, she was searching for her own bedroom in her country house . . . or perhaps she had completely regressed and in her child's mind was searching for something else, or was lost. There had been no trace tonight of that arrogant little girl I had thought about some days before; it was a lonely, depressed Mother that I saw. One could dismiss the matter by calling it hallucination or somnambulism, but there was something in Mother's actions that, although not quite normal, bespoke a certain sense of purpose. Seeing Mother in this light, I felt I could no longer leave her as she was.

As it happened, Mother cut short her stay after twenty days and went home. When we brought her to Tokyo, I had hoped to care for her for at least a month, but I now

127

questioned the wisdom of keeping her any longer and asked Shikako to make arrangements to allow her to return home earlier. We did not tell Mother about it until the morning of her departure.

A few days before she left, the plum tree to the side of my study burst into bloom, and perhaps it was the sight of the white blossoms that started Mother's incessant chatter about the plum groves at her country home. The essence of what she said was that the whole area behind the storehouse was a plum grove, with red as well as white plum trees, which must be a spectacular sight now, at the height of their bloom. As she immediately forgot her own words, she repeated herself over and over. The garden she alluded to was not really large enough to be called a grove, but during the early years of Taisho (1912–26), there had been many plum trees there. Now only a few of the original trees remained, and the storehouse itself was no longer standing.

Well, Mother was finally returning to her house with the plum grove. Soko had stayed overnight, and she and I accompanied Mother. We left in the morning when she was comparatively clearheaded, and she was in great spirits throughout the ride. In response to Soko's question as to whether she knew her destination, Mother replied cheerfully that she didn't know because she was senile, but most probably she was heading for home. It was beyond Soko and me to guess whether she actually did not know or whether she was feigning ignorance.

As might be expected, Mother looked happy when we arrived in Izu and she roamed about the house. By the time we had eaten lunch and gone into the garden together, she no longer had a clear memory of her return from Tokyo that day. Several plum trees were scattered about the unkempt garden, some with red blooms, others with white. All the trees were now old and had few blossoms, and what blossoms there were looked faded. Mother walked about the garden of our country house, this garden so different from the one she had boasted about while in Tokyo. It was most likely the garden of her childhood days to which she had fiercely wished to return, but that desire could not be fulfilled.

"Granny, you kept talking about plum groves but the plum grove is gone, isn't it?" I said.

She nodded her head. "That's so. It's ruined now," she said gravely.

It was hard to ascertain how much she meant of what she said, but as she stood in this decaying garden she gave the impression that she was reminiscing about the glory of times long gone.

That night I gave Shikako and her husband a summary of Mother's behavior in Tokyo. When I broached the topic of Mother's nocturnal activities, Shikako remarked, "She does that here, too. If she did that only once a night in Tokyo, she must have been restraining herself. Here she gets up two, even three times, comes to look into our room, goes to the kitchen, walks through the storeroom, down the hallway, and returns to her own bedroom."

Faced with this information, Yoshiko's assumption that Mother was searching for her own bedroom in her own home did not stand up. Our discussion ventured on why she continued her nocturnal wandering.

"I wonder what it's all about," Shikako mused. "This never happened before . . . only from about a year ago. At first I thought she might be concerned about the doors not being locked, but that doesn't seem to be the case. Recently I have the feeling that perhaps Granny has become a child and is looking for her own mother. She peers into our room and she sees me, but it's as if I'm not the right person, for she barely glances at me, then leaves. Wasn't that the case in Tokyo? A child desperately searching for its mother often has that look."

As she said this I recalled that on the two occasions when Mother visited me late at night, I, too, had seen this look. Although she seemed to have seen me, I could not really be certain of it. She had glanced at me, then quickly turned away. Indeed, on being told this was the look of a child in search of its mother, I was inclined to agree. I was rather startled to know that Shikako had been experiencing Mother's nocturnal visits for some time. That was something I had not been aware of.

"I see her somewhat differently from Shikako," said Akio, Shikako's husband. "I really think she's a mother searching for her child. Do you remember the time she thought that you, as an infant, had disappeared, and she rushed out causing a commotion? This nocturnal roaming began about that time. What I think is that she's wandering around looking for her child. During that previous incident she called for you by name and she might have been

130

searching for the newborn you, but I think it's different now. She's not searching for a particular child, just a child in general, like a mother cat searching for its kittens. That's my impression. I think that a child searching for its mother has a certain poignant expression, which is absent in Granny's case. Instead, there is a certain grimness about her. That is definitely the look of a mother searching for her child." Thus Akio, another daily observer of Mother, also had his opinion.

"But Granny is not just grim. There's a certain pathetic quality about her, too," Shikako protested. "When I watch her from behind as she walks around, I first feel poignancy. I really do think that she is like a child looking for its mother. And, if I could choose between the two, I'd rather have her be the child."

"Well, yes, she would be easier to handle if she became a child," Soko remarked. "Even so, I wonder which she is—a child searching for its mother or a mother looking for her child . . . there's no way to find out other than asking Granny herself."

"What complicates things is that even if we were to ask her, she wouldn't know. 'I don't know. I don't remember doing any such thing,'" Shikako mimicked Mother's manner of speaking.

"That's true," Soko acknowledged. "She probably does not know. Granny is not really conscious of what she's doing. I can't help thinking that her spirit somehow leaves her body and floats around. Last night I slept in the same room with her, and in the middle of the night she got up.

Since I don't often see her like this I decided to accompany her, and it definitely seemed to me that it was only her spirit tottering around. It wasn't as if she was being blown by the wind or anything like that, but rather as if she was being propelled by some force unknown to herself."

"Don't say such creepy things," Shikako said.

"Let's stop now," Soko agreed. "I start feeling sad when we talk like this. I become awfully sorry for her." Apparently the rest felt the same, and we changed the subject.

When Soko spoke of Mother's spirit being moved by some force, I wanted to respond that the force was probably something like instinct, but I stopped myself because I thought that observation would definitely lead to a depressing discussion. It was clear that if we let ourselves feel sorry for Mother, we would feel sad.

Was our child-mother a child searching for her mother or a mother searching for her child, or was she roaming around for some other reason, searching for something else? Whatever her quest, it was certainly something of which Mother herself was unaware, as Soko had said, and unconscious of doing. In that case, I thought the exact nature of Mother's compulsion could be understood in terms of instinct or something akin to it. A mother's need to seek her child and a child's need to find its mother were innate drives, and some of this drive still lingered within my senile mother's being, impelling her toward this strange behavior. Even if I could not comprehend the source of this impulse fully, I could explain her nocturnal activities to myself by this reasoning.

132

Some years before, Mother had gone through a phase of appearing to react only to "the pain of parting from loved ones" in her relationship with others, but now she no longer seemed involved even in that. Her senility had progressed to such a point that I suspected she might be responding solely to a flickering blue flame of instinct that burned somewhere within her decaying body and mind. And if so, then it was not merely depressing but unbearable to think of her in that way. When we, her children, put a sudden stop to our discussion of Mother, my impression was that not only I but also Akio, Shikako, and Soko—each from a different perspective—had glimpsed that flickering blue flame.

Surprisingly, that night, perhaps because she was in her own home for the first time in a long while or because she did not have to demand to be taken there, she slept through the night.

In June of the following year I received a letter from Shikako announcing that her second daughter was about to give birth, and as it was this daughter's first confinement Shikako wanted her home for the event. She would find it difficult to care for both a pregnant woman and Granny; therefore, would we be good enough to take Mother in for about twenty days before and after the birth? This message arrived fifteen months after the time I stood in the upstairs room of the country house musing about the blue flame of instinct flickering in Mother's body. In the intervening months I had gone home on numerous occasions, and each time Mother's condition remained unchanged. There were times when she was relatively clearheaded and also times when her mind was extremely vague. She continued her nocturnal wanderings in the Izu house. Neither Akio nor Shikako spoke any longer of a child searching for its mother or a mother seeking her child. Instead, Shikako was saying what a terrible thing senility was, and since she was Granny's daughter she feared she might end up the same way.

In mid-June Mitsu and I went to the country to get Mother. We stayed for two nights, observing and learning about Mother's current condition from Shikako and her husband. Then on the third morning, equipped with this necessary general information, we got Mother into the car, seating her between us. Although there was nothing particularly wrong with Mother when we got her into the car, she appeared to have shrunk a size and looked more fragile than ever. The car sped along the Kano River, came out at Mishima, and got onto the Tokyo–Nagoya Highway from the Numazu interchange. We rested twice along the way at drive-in restaurants, once at the Numazu interchange and again off the highway near Atsugi. Seated in the corner of an empty restaurant, Mother looked tiny. On both occasions she scooped up ice cream with a small spoon and said, with each mouthful, how "tasty" it was, as if she had never eaten ice cream before. This was her only comment from the time we left the country until we reached Tokyo.

When we arrived home Mother seemed unsettled, as if

she found the surroundings unfamiliar, but she did not immediately demand to go home and she was compliant with members of the family. She took her bath, then had dinner with everyone. She refused to say that she liked anything that was placed before her. If someone asked her, "Wasn't that a tasty dish?" she merely responded with "I guess so." Her manner was somewhat sullen, as if she were thinking, "Since I can't help what's going on I won't complain to you." That night she went to bed early and slept soundly until morning. Yoshiko slept in the adjacent room, separated only by sliding papered doors.

Shikako had told us that Mother was not wandering about at night now as much as before, that she seldom got up more than once during the night and some nights not at all. Shikako said in either case she herself would get up because she wanted to check on Mother, and it was wearing on her.

On the second and third nights of her stay in Tokyo, Mother did not walk about in other rooms; when she did waken, she only awoke Yoshiko to take her to the bathroom. Yoshiko, however, thought that Mother seemed to want to continue her nocturnal roaming but was unsure of her bearings. Since her previous visit Mother's stamina had deteriorated, and the compulsion to walk around whenever she pleased had also vanished.

Four or five days after Mother's arrival, Yoshiko came up with a fresh viewpoint. "It could be that Granny thinks she's in prison here. That's why she's resigned to not wandering about."

Yoshiko reported that on her way back from the bathroom the previous night, Mother had stood in front of my younger son's bedroom and tried to open the door, but it was locked from the inside. Had Mother confused this door with her own? She then muttered to Yoshiko, "They won't let me out anywhere, will they?"

"I didn't think much of it at the time," Yoshiko went on, "but on reflection I believe Granny does this from time to time. And each time she probably thinks that she is being confined."

I thought it pathetic that Mother should have such an illusion, but if it prevented her from wandering about I felt we must let her bear this burden.

As during her previous visit, Mother soon began her daily demands to be taken home, but there was very little energy in those demands. When the thought occurred to her she repeatedly asked to go home, but she usually remained seated on the tatami mats in the living room and seldom made any attempt to go to the front door. In this, too, I sensed a diminishing stamina and, with it, a loss of force in her obsession. At times she showed anger both verbally and nonverbally, but in most cases these moments were the result of hurt pride. Since the reasons for this were never clear, however, it was extremely difficult for the family to deal with. She would listen to neither persuasion nor explanation, but I could clearly detect the arrogant little girl indulged by her grandfather at such times. When someone called her "pig-headed Granny," she looked away with an expression of extreme contempt and sat with both hands placed primly on her lap, reminding me of my five-year-old granddaughter.

Despite such incidents, we all agreed it would not be particularly hard to care for Mother for a month, or even two, at her present level of behavior. We usually opened up our Karuizawa house at the beginning of July, and both Mitsu and I thought we might be able to take Mother that year. My two sons agreed, saying that she might actually enjoy the quiet life in the mountains surrounded by larch trees.

Yoshiko alone was opposed. "Just think about it," she said. "Remember how awful it was last time! Compared to then, Granny's senility is much, much worse. She *won't* think that it's nice and quiet or nice and cool—such feelings are totally gone. The things she *is* thinking and feeling are inconceivable to us," Yoshiko said.

Everyone was silenced. After all, Yoshiko was Mother's main nurse and the one who knew her current condition best, at least her night behavior.

After giving the matter some more thought, it occurred to me that the problem of transportation alone was enough to rule out taking Mother to Karuizawa. As I envisioned the hustle and bustle of the train station I thought it would simply be too hard on her nerves, and a four- or five-hour drive by car would be too harsh on her delicate physique.

When a week, then ten days, went by and Mother's stay in Tokyo continued without serious disruption, I began to feel that Mother was not yielding altogether to the flickering flame of instinct and that Tokyo might be a better place for her than her country home. She did not become the frantic searching mother or the pathetic searching child, if only because she could no longer roam about at night even if she wanted to. With this thought I felt another kind of compassion for her. As she sat quietly in a corner of the living room it occurred to me that she resembled both a little girl who had resigned herself to not finding her mother, and a young mother who had finally given up searching for her child. Her face was at once that of a lonely child and of a bereft mother. When I saw her as a child, she had a child's face, and when I saw her as a mother, she had a mother's face.

About half a month into Mother's stay, I asked her into my study, and we sat across from each other on the veranda facing the lawn. We had just finished a late breakfast, and it was a little past ten. I wished to drink some tea with her before starting work. Yoshiko brought some weak tea for Mother and some strong green tea for me. As I lifted my cup, Mother, who had been glancing at my desk, suddenly said, "That man who's been writing there every day has died, hasn't he?"

"That man" could be none other than myself. "When did he die?" I asked Mother, watching her closely.

She seemed to ponder for a bit, then said somewhat uncertainly, "Perhaps three days ago; today is probably the third day," she said.

I glanced around my study to see how it looked on the third day after I purportedly had died. The room was in complete disorder. Books were crammed indiscriminately into shelves and several piles of books stood on the tatami mats; some of the books had fallen over, others were on the verge of toppling. Scattered among those piles were two suitcases; three cardboard cartons; and several tied-up bundles of reference material, some of it mine, some borrowed. On the window ledge were more reference materials, envelopes, and magazines in untidy piles, while the veranda where we sat was also cluttered with various objects. I thought that should I die with things in such a state, my family would have quite a time clearing up the mess.

My glance swept the room, roving from one area to the next, then stopped at my desk. The top was also in disorder, but as I had not yet started to work, half of it was cleared—and that area alone looked inordinately clean. The housekeeper had pushed things to one side and dusted only that section. In that tidy space were two clean ashtrays and an inkwell arranged in a row. It was with some emotion that I gazed at the desk whose owner allegedly had died.

"So it's three days," I remarked.

"As you know, there are many visitors," Mother said.

"To be sure," I replied.

In fact, the amount of commotion now going on in this home would be what one would expect on the third day after the death of the head of the household. In the adjacent living room Mitsu was talking with two or three people, possibly bankers, and their voices could be heard. In the family room were four members of the family of Mitsu's younger sister; they had stayed overnight and should now be making preparations to leave, although we could not hear their voices. There was also a young couple who had come to meet these relatives. In a corner of the garden two young workers, who had come to repair the garage door, were talking with our housekeeper. I could see them from the veranda.

Just then it occurred to me that Mother was at that moment living within her "circumstantial sense." I am not sure whether there is such a term or, if so, whether my use of it is appropriate, but I thought that there were several pieces of sense-related data that could lead Mother to deduce that this was the third day following the death of the head of the household. My desk showed a degree of tidiness suggestive of about three days' passing since the owner last sat there, and the comings and goings of people seemed in keeping with the third day after a death. In addition, Mother might have picked up many other similar pieces of data unknown to me, and on the basis of those data might be creating her own drama and living in it. In a word, Mother was now living in a home where the head of the family had passed away three days ago; she could observe the mourning period and she could accept death. In the drama that she had invented, she could assign herself any role that took her fancy.

As I pursued this train of thought, Mother's world of senility suddenly acquired a new dimension. I recalled times when, shortly after breakfast, she was convinced that it was close to dusk, and other times when she mistook evening for morning. Whether it was actually morning or evening was immaterial to her; what mattered was that if something made her suppose it was morning, then it was morning; and if something gave her the impression it was evening, then it was evening.

As I sat across from her drinking my tea I wanted to say, "Granny, you've really started something now, haven't you? Now you are well and truly beginning to live in your own world." It definitely was her own world—a world of her own making—in which no one else could enter. Using her senses she had plucked out a slice of reality from life and used it to create another world.

In reply, Mother might have said that this was not the beginning, that she had been living like this for a long time. It was true that she had been confusing evening and morning for some years.

That incident ended, but another rather like it occurred a few weeks later. One day in the beginning of July, Mitsu and our housekeeper loaded a lot of luggage into the car and left for Karuizawa to open up the house and prepare it for summer occupancy. Just before they left, Mother accosted Mitsu at the front door and said, "I have something to say to you." She spoke in a formal tone. When Mitsu turned to enter the house Mother told her that they could talk outside, and she thereupon put on her wooden clogs and preceded Mitsu out of the house. Mother did not go to the front gate, but instead opened the wooden gate that led into the garden. Mitsu followed her. Mother went to the corner of the garden by the lilac bush and made this prefacing statement.

"I've meant to tell you this for some time."

After a pause, she said, "The woman that I live with in my country home is not a relative but a stranger. I thought it best that only you be aware of this." That was the sum of Mother's business with Mitsu.

I learned about it from Mitsu when she returned from Karuizawa the following evening. "Granny was serious," she said. "The way she put it was, 'This is something I wouldn't tell anyone else, but since we are parting and won't see each other again, I'll tell you now.' That person she lives with in the country, it's Shikako, isn't it? Poor thing! Granny's eldest daughter, and she's being made out to be a stranger without any blood ties."

My thoughts returned to the time when I was presumed dead. I had been seen as a dead person and now Mitsu had been seen as a person from whom Mother was parting. Mitsu had spent that morning making preparations to go to Karuizawa, had called the caretakers there to make the arrangements, and had been busy in many ways, and I think Mother got the impression that Mitsu was leaving for a long journey and the two would not meet again soon. The fact that Mitsu had cleaned the family altar before leaving probably gave rise to special reactions in Mother, and Mitsu's conversations with two groups of visitors at the front door may have further stimulated Mother's imagination in ways we could not possibly imagine. In any case, Mother concluded Mitsu was going away and she did what she thought was necessary before Mitsu's departure. In this, Mother again assumed a role and played her part in a drama of her own creation.

A few days later these activities of Mother's were the topic of conversation in our family room. Yoshiko brought up an experience with her Hiroshima grandmother several years before. This grandmother was Mitsu's mother, who in the year before she died at the age of eighty-four, had visited us in Tokyo. On one occasion during her visit, this grandmother waited until no one else was around to give Yoshiko a five-hundred-yen note.

"I told her I didn't want it," Yoshiko recalled, "but in the end I had to accept it. I don't know how to describe it, but Granny looked desperate then. Her eyes were imploring; they seemed to plead with me to accept it. I had to accept it. If I hadn't, I think Granny would have burst into tears."

This was the first I'd heard about that incident. The Hiroshima grandmother was not as senile as Mother, but despite this fact there were clear indications of senility during her last years. I thought that all senile women must enter the same kind of world. I don't know what kind of drama this grandmother had made up about those around her, but she, like Mother, had created a world that no outsider could understand.

"They may be similar in that aspect," one of my sons said, "but our Izu Granny and our Hiroshima Granny were quite different. Izu Granny made our father out to be a dead man and our mother someone who was leaving her. There's some sort of mean streak in her. In that respect, our Hiroshima Granny was less devious. I don't think our Izu Granny would ever offer pocket money to her granddaughter."

143

"There are individual differences in senility, aren't there? Our Izu Granny would be Shingeki (modern drama), while our Hiroshima Granny would be Shimpa (classical drama)," another son added.

Mother's stay in Tokyo ended in less than a month. Shikako called to say that her younger daughter had safely delivered a son and would soon leave for her own home. Mother could return any time. For two nights running Shikako had dreamed of Mother and was worried.

The call came at an opportune moment, for it was already time for us to leave for Karuizawa, and if Mother could not come with us we could not allow her to stay on in Tokyo, with the thermometer climbing each day. Soko agreed to take Mother to the country and on her return, after seeing Mother safely home, she said, "Granny has become very good, hasn't she? When she's too good, I become all the more concerned about her. She has forgotten everything. I even wonder now whether she has forgotten the fact that she is senile."

About seven months after Mother left Tokyo—at the end of February in the following year—her children, grandchildren, and close relatives celebrated Mother's eighty-eighth birthday. It was the February of the year prior to her death. Mother's birthday actually fell on February 15, but to fit the schedule of those who were working, it was delayed for ten days. We reserved the banquet room of the hot-springs inn in our hometown for the party. Her sons, her daughters, their spouses, her grandchildren, and great-grandchildren—twenty-four people in all—assembled for

acknowledged this with a brief, polite smile and immediately looked away. Her whole aura was gloomy and joyless.

Halfway through the party, the photographer arrived to take commemorative pictures and Shikako brought out a red head covering and a red sleeveless kimono jacket for Mother. Mother stubbornly refused to put on these strange red things. After being admonished by Shikako, she finally allowed the head covering to be placed on her and let herself be wrapped in the kimono jacket, but only for the picture-taking. (It was no wonder she disliked them—they did not become her.) As soon as the pictures were taken, she got rid of the garments with a slightly irritated gesture; in her mind they were clearly not meant for human wear.

I was the host of this banquet, but I did not interfere with its procedure. That I had delegated to the younger people. Everyone, except Mother, appeared to be having a good time, and as the party gradually became more festive I became more concerned that she alone was not enjoying it.

Perhaps she had returned to the sumptuous and extravagant world of her early girlhood and a part of her viewed the present festivities as a meager banquet no matter what was being celebrated and refused to accept any part of it. Or it may be that she had picked up data from the somewhat excited atmosphere of the past few days in preparation for her birthday celebration, and from that created a drama in which she was playing quite a different role from what we intended for her. Whatever the case, however, I was not particularly displeased with Mother's gloomy behavior throughout the banquet, for I thought it

146

very much in character and reassuringly consistent with the self she had recently been projecting.

The day after the party, which from Mother's viewpoint could hardly have been called a roaring success, we, her children, assembled in the family home for the first time in a long while. The mother who had looked so unhappy at the party was now all smiles as she sat surrounded by her sons and daughters. No one could figure out what had happened to her mood.

By now Mother's physical and mental deterioration was obvious to all. She seldom said anything, and although she kept repeating herself when she did speak, she now muttered, as if talking to herself, and the repetitions were not so conspicuous. Further, once she sat down, she did not move. It seemed to cost her a great deal of effort to change her seat, and she remained where she was even when others got up and left. This would have been unthinkable behavior for Mother a few years before.

"Thanks to her change, I have been freed from Granny these days," said Shikako. "The intervals between the times she wakes up at night have lengthened and it's now once in so many days. When she does get up, she's like a ghost. You know, her movements are slow and she really does look ghostly coming into our bedroom. Before, she used to follow me around all day: when I went to the kitchen she followed me, when I went to the front door she came with me, but that stopped abruptly. In fact, sometimes when I realize Granny's not behind me I'm startled."

That day we all wanted to keep Mother company and we brought up the topic of Father's military posts where Mother had lived for some years. Taipei, Kanazawa, Hirosaki—these were mainly the places that were discussed.

At times her daughters asked her whether she knew a particular person, or my brother or I told her she probably wouldn't remember a certain person. She had forgotten almost everyone, but at times she said, "Oh, yes, she was a good person. She was a good, kind person. She didn't have any children and I wonder what she's doing now."

Mother recalled three or four such people, and when she did her face lit up momentarily. It was as if a ray of light had suddenly pierced the damaged brain, and it astonished us. We could tell, from her expression alone, whether the name and the person matched. And when they did, she repeated the same stereotyped phrases, "Yes, that was a good person; that was a kind person."

In contrast, when she could not recall the person mentioned she remained silent and shook her head or made a spiteful remark. "She probably wasn't much of a person anyway." Apparently she meant that if she didn't remember a person it was because that person wasn't worth remembering.

"That's just like Granny, isn't it?" Soko said. "She ignores her own memory and blames the other party."

"Observing Granny, I think that when people become senile they regard their own children as strangers, with no blood ties whatsoever," my brother said with emotion. "The children think, because it is their own parent, that they will be the last ones to be forgotten, but this is purely sentimental. She's forgotten about me long ago. Naturally, when we are face to face like this she seems to believe I'm her son. When I tell her my name, she appears to remember that that was her son's name, but she doesn't put me and the name together. For some reason, I'm the very first one to have been totally and completely forgotten by Granny."

"Speaking of that," Shikako chimed in, "I have lived with Granny for ten years and taken care of her, and I don't know when this happened, but she no longer thinks of me as her daughter, either. She takes me for an older servant. As you know, she keeps calling me Grandmother. I think that's very impudent but, well, it can't be helped."

In reality, Shikako had drawn the worst lot. If Mother had forgotten Shikako, then naturally she had also forgotten Akio. In Soko's case and mine, for some reason, she had thought of us as her son and daughter until relatively recently, but that, too, had gradually become uncertain in the last few years, and at some unknown time we, too, had been placed among the forgotten.

"Whether we're forgotten early or late, well, it comes to the same thing at the end," I said. "We need harbor no bitter feelings now that we are all equally forgotten. We've all been finally abandoned by our own mother. But remember, Father was also rejected by her. Senility is a frightening thing."

We didn't know when Mother forgot about Father; by the time we were aware of it, Father's existence had already become a shadowy flicker in her memory. To borrow my brother's words, Mother's senility had deprived even Father, the man with whom she had shared a long life, of any special regard and placed him on an equal footing with others.

"On the other hand, Granny remembers many people from the distant past, doesn't she? And she seems to recall them quite clearly," said Soko.

"She remembers those who were kind to her or those she thought were good people, and she seems to have forgotten all the others who didn't fit into those categories," my brother said. "By that definition we, her sons and daughters, are neither kind nor good people."

"I wonder if that's so."

"That's what I think, and I've believed it for quite a while. Because of Granny's personality, I think she has always reacted strongly. 'Ah, that's a very kind person!' 'Ah, that's a gentle soul!' 'Ah, what unpleasant things that person does!' or 'What disagreeable things that person says!' I think there's no denying she felt those things more strongly than others. Therefore, I believe that in her mind she awarded gold stars to those she thought were good and kind, while she struck off her list the names of those she thought of as being otherwise. Whether she gave a gold star or crossed off a name would not matter in the least if she hadn't become senile, but fortunately or unfortunately, she is completely senile. And after she became senile she forgot first those whose names she had crossed off. If there was some sort of order in her forgetting, well, I'd say in general she forgot them one after the other from the top of the list she'd made."

"In that case, then, we have all been crossed off."

"We have *actually* been crossed off. When I send out New Year's cards I sometimes delete the names of those that I think I don't need to write to any longer. Well, I think it must be something like that."

"Then we are among those that have been crossed off. At some point our names were struck out, too?"

"Of course, with a firm stroke."

"I wonder when that was."

"Well, that's hard to say," my brother said.

He spoke half-jokingly, but listening to him gave me food for thought. It is true that as a person goes through life he enters and crosses off in his address book the names of people he encounters.

"Well, then, when do you think your name was crossed out by Granny?" Shikako asked my brother.

"Well, there was the time when I argued with Mother about my job. It might have been then when I was young."

"That was long ago, wasn't it?"

"Even so, I think my name was crossed off then. If Granny had not become senile it would have been only a matter of my *name* being deleted, but since she's senile it is *I* who have been erased."

As I listened to my brother, I thought that if there had been a time when his name was crossed off, it most likely would have been when he married into another family and took their surname. Mother had approved heartily of the match and displayed much enthusiasm, but when the marriage actually took place and it came time for her own child to leave her for another family, might she not have suddenly felt abandoned—especially as it was my brother whom she had liked most? If Mother had crossed off my brother's name it must have been then.

"Then what about Father?" Soko asked.

"That was probably around the time the war ended," I responded.

If Father's name had been crossed off by Mother's hand, I thought, it could have happened at no other time. I think that when the prestige and power which had been his during all his adult years as a military officer were suddenly stripped away from him without ado at the end of the war, and he became a worthless outcast in a defeated nation, Mother probably wanted to tell him that this was not what she had bargained for. During active military service Father had been quite a tyrant with Mother, but she served him well despite his behavior; and in contrast to his sudden social withdrawal after retirement, she accepted the presidency of the Military Wives Association in our hometown and performed functions befitting the wife of a military officer. Because of her pride and competitiveness, Father's loss of prestige had undoubtedly come as a great blow to her. Perhaps there was a part of her that wanted to rebel against him. If she had crossed him off, it must have been around that time.

"If that's so, then Soko's husband and I must have been crossed off about that time, too," Akio said. Akio also had been a military man, and Soko's husband had been a medical officer.

"I wonder when you were crossed off?" Soko asked me.

"Perhaps when I married Mitsu. If not then, it must have been when I refused to be a doctor and became a reporter. When I told Mother I was going to become a reporter, she didn't look at all happy," I said.

Our acquired family line, which for generations was professionally committed to medicine, was changed by me. My decision not to enter medical school was undoubtedly incomprehensible to Mother, who had been convinced that hers was a distinguished family of physicians ever since she went to live with her grandfather. If there was another time when she might have crossed off my name—and there may have been—I was simply not aware of it. Perhaps my brother, Shikako, Akio, and Soko had also been crossed off at times unknown to them.

As we speculated in a rather heated manner, Mother, the center of it all, was asleep in a chair in the next room with her handkerchief covering her upturned face. She may be senile, I thought, but the way she protects herself even in sleep has always been very much in character for her; this trait might be one her children would find difficult to equal.

From the fall of the year of Mother's eighty-eighth birthday to the following spring, I visited my hometown three times, and on each occasion Mother appeared to have shrunk further in size. I always found her in the room facing the inner courtyard, her tiny body huddled beneath the foot warmer cover. During cold weather, of course, she warmed her body there, but even when there was no need for it she remained huddled against it. At night her bedding was placed beside the foot warmer, and there she slept. Mother rarely left that area. Previously, if she spotted a single fallen leaf in the garden she promptly went after it and, in general, would scarcely sit still for a moment. Now, however, it appeared to be a great effort for her even to move.

Mother came to the family room only at mealtimes to sit at the dining table, but the amount she consumed was so minimal it seemed a wonder she could stay alive. There was always a little platter for her with a very small portion of sweet beans boiled tender, and she reached only in that direction. She ate absolutely no meat, vegetables, or fruit. She had been finicky in her tastes ever since childhood, and with her advancing senility this tendency became more pronounced: if she disliked something she totally ignored it. "Granny is happy as long as she has omelettes and boiled beans," said Shikako. "I'm sure that when she was small she ate only those things."

Moreover, Mother became even less talkative, and when she was silent it was difficult to tell the degree of her senility. Occasionally a visitor sat by her foot warmer. Mother never recognized the person beside her, but she smiled pleasantly and made such remarks as, "It looks like good weather today," or "How are you doing?" She had become extremely cautious about revealing her senility to others.

Even with her declining stamina, Mother was seldom incontinent, and when she did have an accident there was always hot-springs water in the small bathroom, piped in from the ravine. Thus it was relatively simple for Shikako to take care of her. In any event, it seemed likely that Mother would try to remedy her occasional accidents herself, for she had not lost her desire to take care of this herself.

When I went home at New Year's and saw Mother's state, the thought occurred to me that I should not be surprised if she were to go at any time. Akio voiced similar thoughts. But the women—Shikako, Mitsu, Soko—all held the view that Mother might well continue to live on in the same condition for a few years.

From May to June of that year, I went on a trip to Afghanistan, Iran, and Turkey. Before I left I had thought of going to see Mother, and I notified Shikako and her husband of the date of my homecoming. But when the day came, and after I had actually made arrangements for a taxi, I decided to cancel the trip. I somehow saw it as a farewell visit, and thus I felt it would be safer not to go. I telephoned Shikako about my decision, told her the reason, and requested, if anything were to happen to Mother while I was away, that she discuss matters with Mitsu and Soko and handle all necessary arrangements.

"I don't think anything untoward will happen to Granny," Shikako said. "All last night she slept very well, and this morning I even went to check on her twice because she slept so late. Her skin tone has become very lustrous, like a young girl's. *I* look much more like an old woman."

When I returned from that trip at the end of June the rainy season had not yet ended. My fatigue after the rugged trip by car to various desert outposts and frontier lands was such that I was not my usual self for the whole summer. In August I went to Karuizawa to escape the heat, but even there I was plagued by sleepless nights. It was not until September that I fully recovered. Then one day I looked up from the veranda of my study in Tokyo at a beautifully clear autumn sky, and I suddenly wanted to visit the country home.

Half a year had elapsed since I had last been there, but Mother looked no different from that time. As usual, I found her seated in the room facing the inner courtyard in front of the foot warmer. She greeted me as she would a stranger. Just as Shikako had said, her complexion was lustrous, and when she spoke she looked embarrassed. In these ways she gave the impression that she was more young girl than old woman.

I stayed two nights there. On the second night I had come downstairs and was walking along the corridor toward the bathroom when I encountered Mother coming from the opposite direction. In her night clothes she had the form appropriate for her age, and her face was also that of an old woman.

"It's snowing, isn't it?" she remarked.

I was startled. I told her there was no snow, and a sudden humiliation came over her face as if she had been censured.

156

Then she said again, this time in a whisper, "It's snowing, isn't it?"

I walked with her back to her bedroom and, without entering her room, went on to the bathroom. Although I knew it could not possibly be snowing, I opened the bathroom window and looked out. It was pitch dark outside, but stars were visible in one section of the sky and I could hear the cicadas singing in the bushes in the back garden.

On my way back to my room I looked again into Mother's room. Her bedding had been laid out but Mother had not gotten inside; instead she was seated in her usual daytime place in front of the foot warmer. Although she did not appear to be cold in her night clothes, I picked up the kimono that was folded beside her pillow and placed it around her shoulders. I then sat down on the other side of the foot warmer, facing her. I was curious to know what had caused this latest hallucination. Before I could speak, Mother again said, "It's snowing, isn't it? Everything is covered with snow."

"Do you feel it's snowing?" I asked gently.

"But it *is* snowing."

"It isn't snowing. The stars are out."

Mother's expression revealed that she didn't believe what I said could possibly be true. She started to say something, apparently failed to find suitable words, and fell silent. Then after an interval she said again, gravely, "It's snowing, isn't it?" Now she listened intently as if waiting for a sound outside. Imitating her, I also listened intently. There

157

was no sound either outdoors or in the house. Shikako and her husband were in their own room and probably sleeping since it was already well past eleven. Somehow at night this country home, which long ago had served as a busy clinic for Mother's grandfather (and my great-grandfather), had now begun to feel empty, untenanted, although it was not particularly large.

I thought Mother must at this moment be living in her "circumstantial sense," just as she was that time in Tokyo. As we faced each other over the unheated foot warmer, I thought that the quiet that enveloped us could be interpreted as the hush of a snowy night. Even so, Mother could not have experienced a snowy night for over forty years. Some of Father's military posts had been snowy places—Asahigawa, Kanazawa, and Hirosaki—but Mother had been twenty-two or twenty-three when they were stationed in Asahigawa, and Kanazawa and Hirosaki had been their posts close to the time of Father's retirement. Father had retired from military service at Hirosaki, and that had been over forty years before.

"Do you remember Hirosaki?" I asked her. "In Hirosaki, it snowed every day during January, didn't it?"

Mother merely looked puzzled. It was the same when I asked about Kanazawa and Asahigawa.

"Yes, that's so. It did snow," she finally remarked, but it was clear she was just mouthing the words.

I persisted. "Of all the places you went, Granny, the place called Asahigawa had the most snow, didn't it? It snowed night after night."

158

"Is that so? It snowed night after night? Was there such a place?" She tilted her head slightly and seemed to be trying to reach back into her memory. As she concentrated, her expression became extremely pained and sorrowful. Then her face cleared and she said dully, "I have forgotten everything; I've become totally senile."

"It's all right. You don't have to remember," I said.

It was strange how Mother's mannerism as she tried to recall her past—her facial expression, the tilt of her head, eyes cast down at her lap—gave the impression she was being made to do some penance. I felt ashamed. I had no right to make her try to recall the past. Indeed, in Mother's case, trying to pull something out from her memory was probably much like trying to pull a sunken bundle of wood out of a frozen swamp covered by snow. That task would be painful and distressing, and the wood when it finally emerged would drip icy drops of water.

I got Mother into bed and left her room. And later, as I lay in my own bed upstairs, I thought that tonight was probably not the first night Mother had spent in a world where it snowed. Perhaps the night before and the night before that she had heard the sound of falling snow and spent the quiet hours alternately listening and sleeping. And possibly the next day and the day after would end in similar nights.

I wondered whether Mother had now truly reached the epitome of isolation. She was no longer moved by "the pain of parting from loved ones," nor did she trouble herself with the deaths of others or their funeral gifts. The

159

blue flame of instinct which at one time had shone fiercely now burned low and was all but extinguished. Even as she lived in a world of snowy nights, her body and mind had deteriorated too far for her to play a part in the dramas she created. She may have returned to childhood, when she was trained to be an arrogant little girl, but the stage lights had been turned off and all the sets enveloped in night. Not only had she lost her husband, her life's companion, she had also lost two sons and two daughters. Siblings, relatives, acquaintances, intimates—she had lost them all; or perhaps abandoned them all. She now lived alone in the home in which she had been reared, and every night it snowed around her. And now she only watched the surface of the snow, that white snow which was engraved in her mind in her youth and which she now mysteriously evoked out of the distant past.

The following day I rose about nine and ate a late breakfast in the family room. Mother came in, sat on a sofa nearby, looked out toward the garden, and from time to time looked at me. It seemed she wanted to tell me something but didn't quite know what it was.

"I'll come again next month," I said.

"Oh, yes, next month." Mother smiled but she didn't seem to know who I was or what next month was.

At ten a taxi arrived. "Well, Granny, take care of yourself," I said.

"Oh, are you leaving now?" She came to the front door to see me off. I stopped her when she tried to step onto the dirt floor of the entrance and she said, "Well, then, I'll take leave of you here." When I looked back as I entered the car she was still standing on the raised platform above the dirt floor, looking at me while her hands straightened the collar of her kimono. Her manner suggested that she was concentrating very hard on adjusting her collar, as though she couldn't see me off without tidying the disarray of her kimono. That was the last time I saw Mother alive.

It was shortly past noon when Soko and I arrived at our country home. Several relatives and neighbors had gathered in Mother's bedroom and were seated in a circle, as if surrounding an invisible table. The sliding door between that room and the inner living room had been removed, and in the living room a quilt had been laid out, on which were laid Mother's remains. Three or four other relatives were present in the living room as I entered, and after nodding to them I went to sit by Mother's body. It was a beautiful doll's face that I saw. The slight curve of Mother's lips affected an expression she had worn as a young woman. I touched her face and held her hands. She was as cold as ice.

Shikako came up beside me and said, "Aren't her hands cold. Touch them a bit; they will soon warm up." I did as I was told, and I felt my body warmth transferred to the skin and bone of Mother's hands, which were as white as if they had been bleached, the veins making blue traces against the white.

Toward evening, a young Buddhist priest from a village

several miles away came for the ceremonial sutra readings prior to the placing of the body in the casket. At seven, Mitsu and my eldest daughter arrived from Tokyo, and after they had burned incense Mother was put in her casket. The female relatives swathed her arms and legs in white wrappings and placed a white covering on her head. Unlike the red head covering she had worn on her eighty-eighth birthday, the white one suited her well. She was the picture of one setting forth on a journey. Shikako placed a short dagger at Mother's breast; Soko, Mitsu, and the grandchildren surrounded her face with chrysanthemums.

That night a wake was held. Soko's daughter and son-in-law were there. This son-in-law was a young psychiatrist who had come to visit Mother in Izu from time to time during the past two years, and on each occasion he had examined her. I thought the relative tranquillity of her last years was largely the result of this young man's ministrations, and I thanked them both, my niece and her husband, on Mother's behalf.

This young doctor had last called about ten days before to examine Mother, and he said he had not at that time expected a drastic change in her condition. Then he told us the results of that particular examination.

"At the end," he said laughingly, "Granny really gave it to me. After I completed the examination and we were all drinking tea in Granny's room, Granny looked at me and asked my wife, who was seated beside me, who 'that person' was. My wife told her I was the doctor who had just examined her, and Granny said softly, speaking to no one in particular, 'There are all kinds of doctors.' I was bowled over. She certainly took me down a peg."

I thought that must have been a moment when, from within Mother's drastically withered body—which toward the end could almost be held in one hand—a final flicker of her old spirit suddenly flared.

Two days later, on the twenty-fourth, Mitsu, Soko, Shikako and her husband, and I rose at five. At six I stood in front of Mother's casket, then I stepped aside and watched from the sidelines as friends and relatives came forward and made their final farewells. Mother's face looked very young and very brave then. I used a stone to nail the coffin shut. The coffin was placed on the vehicle used as a hearse, and about twenty relatives and neighbors boarded it. The hearse went onto the Shimoda Highway, left the highway at Shuzen Temple, entered a road that ran along the Omi River, and traveled toward the crematorium through a small ravine heavily forested with maples. The scattered villages in the ravine appeared to be perpetually damp with dew, perhaps because of the shade of the surrounding maples.

When we arrived at the crematorium the priest read a sutra, after which the coffin was immediately placed in the cremation furnace. I followed one of the workers around to the back of the building, reentered through another door, and stood in front of the furnace opening. There, following his directions, I lit an oil-stained rag with a match. Instantaneously, red flames leaped on the other side of the furnace opening and the fire began to roar.

163

We spent about two hours in the waiting room until we were called by the old man in charge. Then we all went and stood before the furnace into which Mother's coffin had been placed. Soon the man pulled out a large, rectangular metal box containing what remained of Mother's bones. We were told that some of those bones should be picked up only by relatives and he set these aside for us with his chopsticks. I picked up the first bone fragment and placed it in a white urn. Each of the other family members picked up a piece, and then I picked up the remaining pieces. After all the fragments had been placed inside the urn, the old man tied it criss-cross with wire, wrapped it in white paper, placed it in a white box, and finally covered it with a piece of gold brocade.

With this package, I entered the hearse last. A place in the rear had been saved for me. I sat down and placed the urn on my lap and held it with both hands. At that moment I thought of Mother and the long, fierce battle she had fought alone. The battle was over now, and she was just so many fragments of bone.

定価3,000円
in Japan